ENGLISH WORKSHOP

FIRST COURSE

TEACHER'S NOTES WITH ANSWER KEYS

HOLT, RINEHART AND WINSTON
Harcourt Brace & Company
Austin • New York • Orlando • Chicago • Atlanta
San Francisco • Boston • Dallas • Toronto • London

Copyright © by Holt, Rinehart and Winston

All rights reserved. No part of this publication may be reproduced or transmitted in any form or by any means, electronic or mechanical, including photocopy, recording, or any information storage and retrieval system, without permission in writing from the publisher.

Requests for permission to make copies of any part of the work should be mailed to the following address: Permissions Department, Holt, Rinehart and Winston, 10801 N. MoPac Expressway, Building 3, Austin, Texas 78759.

HOLT, HRW, and the **"Owl Design"** are trademarks licensed to Holt, Rinehart and Winston, registered in the United States of America and/or other jurisdictions.

Printed in the United States of America

If you have received these materials as examination copies free of charge, Holt, Rinehart and Winston retains title to the materials and they may not be resold. Resale of examination copies is strictly prohibited.

Possession of this publication in print format does not entitle users to convert this publication, or any portion of it, into electronic format.

4 5 6 7 8 9 1410 15 14 13

4500425861

CONTENTS

TEACHER'S NOTES 1

ANSWER KEY: Pupil's Edition
INVITATION TO WRITING
- Chapter 1: The Writing Process 9
- Chapter 2: Paragraph Workshops 10
- Chapter 3: Composition Workshops 10

AIMS FOR WRITING
- Chapter 4: Expressing Yourself 11
- Chapter 5: Creative Writing 11
- Chapter 6: Informing Others 12
- Chapter 7: Persuading Others 13

LANGUAGE AND STYLE
- Chapter 8: Sentence Workshops 13
- Chapter 9: Language Workshops 15

GRAMMAR, USAGE, MECHANICS
- Chapter 10: The Sentence 15
- Chapter 11: Parts of Speech 16
- Chapter 12: Parts of Speech 17
- Chapter 13: Complements 19
- Chapter 14: The Phrase 20
- Chapter 15: The Clause 23
- Chapter 16: Sentence Structure 24
- Chapter 17: Agreement 25
- Chapter 18: Using Verbs Correctly 26
- Chapter 19: Using Pronouns Correctly 28
- Chapter 20: Using Modifiers Correctly 29
- Chapter 21: A Glossary of Usage 30
- Chapter 22: Capital Letters 31
- Chapter 23: Punctuation 32
- Chapter 24: Punctuation 34
- Chapter 25: Spelling 35

ANSWER KEY: Assessment Booklet
PART ONE: GRAMMAR
- Chapter 10: The Sentence 37
- Chapter 11: Parts of Speech 37
- Chapter 12: Parts of Speech 38
- Chapter 13: Complements 38
- Chapter 14: The Phrase 38
- Chapter 15: The Clause 39
- Chapter 16: Sentence Structure 39

PART TWO: USAGE
- Chapter 17: Agreement 40
- Chapter 18: Using Verbs Correctly 40
- Chapter 19: Using Pronouns Correctly 40
- Chapter 20: Using Modifiers Correctly 41
- Chapter 21: A Glossary of Usage 41

PART THREE: MECHANICS
- Chapter 22: Capital Letters 42
- Chapter 23: Punctuation 42
- Chapter 24: Punctuation 42
- Chapter 25: Spelling 43

ENGLISH WORKSHOP—FIRST COURSE

TEACHER'S NOTES

THE AIMS AND MODES OF WRITING

Writing accomplishes something. It gets politicians elected (speeches and commercials) and workers promoted (job evaluations). It soothes pain (a diary) and causes chills (a horror novel). When students see what written language can do *for them*, learning to write becomes not just a school lesson but a life lesson.

Four Basic Aims

To express oneself, to create literature, to inform, to persuade—these four writing purposes, or aims, structure the writing lessons in *English Workshop*.

Expressive Writing. Expressive writing voices the writer's thoughts, feelings, or beliefs. The writing may be private, as in diaries, or public, as in personal essays or statements of faith. The emphasis is on the writer, and the approach is frankly subjective—though a specific piece of writing (relating an experience, for instance) may present data and facts.

Creative Writing. Creative writing uses language inventively to stimulate the thoughts, feelings, and imaginations of readers. While all writing involves originality and imaginative thinking, the term *creative writing* highlights creation in literary forms: novels, plays, and poems, as well as jokes, movies, and popular songs. The emphasis is on imagination and on language itself.

Expository Writing. Expository writing informs or explains. It may also explore complex ideas. Exposition includes news stories, reports, encyclopedia articles, and essays. The writer's emphasis is on the topic; the approach is objective, and the content is factual.

Persuasive Writing. Persuasion seeks to convince. Editorials, ads, sermons, and fund solicitations are all examples of persuasive writing. The emphasis is on the reader or listener, who is urged to accept an idea or to take an action. Because of this emphasis, the credibility of the writer is highly important. He or she must carefully mix factual evidence and emotional appeals.

One Subject: Four Aims

A good way to illustrate for students the differences among the aims is to suggest a single topic and recast it for varying purposes. Let's say the general subject is boys entering a pageant intended for girls: the Miss Hobart High contest, the Homecoming Queen election, the Strawberry Princess competition, and so on.

- **Expressive: A Personal Narrative.** Darryl, in a paper titled "Sexism on All Sides," writes in the first person about entering the Miss Hobart High contest: why he decided to do it, how people reacted, what happened, how he felt as a contestant, and what he learned.

- **Creative: A Limerick.** Darryl recaps his pageant experience in an amusing series of limericks.

- **Informative: A Report.** Darryl researches the trend and reports his findings. He notes similar contests throughout the nation, the stated motives of the young men, and reactions to the young mens' participation.

- **Persuasive: A Letter to the Editor.** Darryl writes to both the school and city newspapers, calling for the abolition of the Miss Hobart High contest. He argues that the contest is sexist (there is no "Mr." Hobart High), demeaning (beauty, rather than intelligence or achievement, is emphasized), frivolous (the winner has no duties), and a waste of funds.

The Communication Process

Concrete examples like the ones above reinforce for students the fundamental elements of verbal communication—a **writer**, a **subject**, an **audience**, and **language**—as well as the dynamic relationships among the four elements. As the purpose changes, the main focus shifts from the writer (Darryl) to language (the poetry), to the subject matter (challenges to traditionally female pageants), to the audience (newspaper readers and their opinions).

The Modes

A knowledge of basic aims is not enough, of course, to make students accomplished writers. Even with a subject, a purpose, and an audience, students have to know something about the forms, or modes, of writing: *narration, description, classification,* and *evaluation*.

In the *English Workshop* lessons, students are guided to write effectively in different modes. In an expressive essay, for example, students may need to use narration. They're prompted to describe situations, to recall vivid sensory details, and to order events chronologically. Students learn how the choices and order of details mark different approaches to a subject—how such choices make for an effective comparison (*classification*), review (*evaluation*), or character sketch (*description*).

THE WRITING PROCESS

Writing is more than the isolated moment of physically putting words on paper. It is the dynamic sum of all the moments of analysis, invention, discovery, decision, and even daydreaming that transpire before a writer says, "I'm finished."

Aspects of the Writing Process

The study of writers and their writing activities has shown a common process composed of a series of stages: **prewriting, writing, evaluating and revising, proofreading and publishing.** The writing process is not inflexible, however. Individual writers develop their own styles and variations of the process. For example, one writer may make extensive prewriting notes, while another may take a walk in the woods and then immediately start writing a first draft.

Researchers have also discovered that the writing process is recursive, not linear. In other words, a writer doesn't necessarily proceed in a straight line from prewriting to drafting to evaluating, and so forth. Quite often the writer doubles back, going from drafting back to prewriting to get more ideas, or from evaluation back to drafting to add missing material.

All writers benefit from an understanding of the writing process. Knowing and practicing the basic steps helps writers (especially beginning writers) become more comfortable with writing and learn to experiment with their own abilities.

Prewriting

Prewriting really means pre*drafting*. Prewriting encompasses finding a topic, considering audience and purpose, generating or gathering ideas, and organizing those ideas. It's a stage that beginning writers may fear, avoid, or shortchange. Often, writers are helped immeasurably just by learning that prewriting *is* part of the writing process.

Ideas. A basic prewriting task is identifying ideas for writing. On pages 1–4, *English Workshop* discusses techniques for finding ideas. Students can use these techniques again and again to generate ideas for subjects or topics and for details related to their topics. Most important, students' topics will reflect their individual interests so that they *own* the writing. To ensure that students are able to refer to these techniques from time to time, they may want to add pages 1–4 to a writing notebook.

Purpose and Audience. Every act of writing has two purposes, a specific one (e.g., to get a refund for a concert ticket) and a general one (e.g., an aim for writing). Chapters 4–7 of *English Workshop* reflect the four basic aims:

- to express oneself
- to create literature
- to inform
- to persuade

> **"**Writing is the dynamic sum of all the moments of analysis, invention, discovery, decision, and even daydreaming that transpire before a writer says, 'I'm finished.'**"**

While a piece of writing can combine aims, one aim almost always predominates; focusing on that primary aim helps students to determine what and how they will write.

Every act of writing has an audience, even if it's only the writer himself or herself. Student writers need to have and believe in an audience other than a teacher. Making an audience real—that is, knowing who they are, what they know and don't know, what they expect, and what they like—guides students in choosing content, vocabulary, sentence style, and tone. A flesh-and-blood audience is one strength of classroom writing groups: Students find out how their peers react to their words. Often, they're surprised!

Organization. With goals decided and information accumulated, the students' next step is organizing. Students assess their information and make a plan, which may be a rough list, a more structured outline, or a graphic device such as a time line or chart. Part of the writing process is learning common organizational techniques (chronological order, order of importance, and so on) that work well with particular types of writing. Each *English Workshop* writing lesson, for example, offers students a visual organizer within which to arrange the paper's details.

Writing

Remind students that drafting is discovery, not the delivery of an error-free paper. Students can follow their written plans but should feel free to make changes and "mistakes." Their object is to get their ideas into sentences and paragraphs. Faulty grammar, usage, and mechanics can be fixed later. *No first draft is a last draft.*

Evaluating and Revising

Now comes a twofold stage: judging, then changing. Writers must evaluate what's wrong (and what's right) in their writing before revising it. In the "Aims for Writing" chapters, the "Questions for Evaluation" portion of each *English Workshop* lesson shows how specific criteria can aid both self-review and peer review. Then students can undertake the basic acts of revision: adding, cutting, replacing, and reordering.

Proofreading and Publishing

Most writers revise more than once. They may even start over, in whole or in part. But with a final, clean copy in hand, the last step is *proofreading*. Students should think of proofreading as a crucial polishing: catching any remaining mistakes in grammar, usage, or mechanics. The "Guidelines for Proofreading" on page 8 in *English Workshop* can be used as a checklist for all papers.

Finally, if the process of writing is to be completed, its result should be *published*. An audience should read (or listen to) what has been written. As the publishing suggestions in the lessons show, students can share their writing in many ways: sending it to a newspaper, reading it aloud to a club, mailing it to someone who helped in the writing, or showing it to another teacher.

STYLES OF LEARNING

People differ in the ways they receive and process information. They tend to channel information through one, or sometimes a combination of two or three, of the learning modalities—auditory, visual, tactile/kinesthetic. For example, students whose main channel for receiving information is auditory would especially benefit from a class discussion of sentence parts. Visual learners might prefer highlighting sentence parts in various colors. Manipulating the parts of sentences on tagboard strips would be an effective method for tactile/kinesthetic learners.

The following chart of patterns of learning shows how students remember information best. If you observe these patterns in your students, you might want to include different learning modalities in your lesson plans.

VISUAL LEARNER	AUDITORY LEARNER	TACTILE/KINESTHETIC LEARNER
Likes written directions	Follows oral directions well	Needs to write directions down
Benefits from movies, slides, or television	Benefits from tapes records, or radio	Benefits from clapping or other rhythm activities
Enjoys drawing, painting, and working with patterns, maps, and diagrams	Enjoys group discussions, telling stories, and hearing other points of view	Enjoys working with hands or body, chalkboard activities, computers, typing, acting, floor games
Responds to facial expressions and body language	Responds to voice tone and rhythm	Responds to body language
Needs written praise, such as comments on papers, self-stick notes	Needs oral praise	Needs appropriate physical rewards, such as a pat on the back

IDEAS FOR ASSESSMENT: HOLISTIC SCORING AND PORTFOLIOS

Every developing writer needs the feedback a teacher can provide by praising, questioning, and helping to identify problems. But attempting to give students feedback can create other problems. First, it can be extremely time-consuming. Second, it can work against students' understanding of writing as a process. Students may become fixated on the end product. Teachers and researchers are finding ways to keep the paper load manageable and to give students solid feedback without focusing attention solely on grades.

Holistic Scoring

Holistic scoring is a method of evaluation that focuses on the *whole* of a student's paper. The evaluator does not write comments or score the work's separate aspects, such as main ideas, organization, or grammar. A single score indicates the level of competence, sometimes using a number (with 0 or 1 the lowest score and 4 or 5 the highest) or a designation (low, average, or high).

Yet holistic scoring, which is also called general impression, is not vague or subjective, because each scoring level has written, descriptive criteria. (For an example, see the scoring scales in the Answer Key for the pupil's edition.)

The first step in effective holistic scoring, then, is determining criteria. While a single scale of basic criteria (content, organization, sentence variety, etc.) may be used for all papers, criteria specific to each assignment give students more information. The scales in the *English Workshop* Answer Key are one source of holistic criteria, and the "Questions for Evaluation" in each lesson are other valuable resources.

While the holistic method won't replace more detailed evaluations, it does have benefits beyond its speed.

- It helps students see writing as a synergistic whole, a total effect not reducible to its parts.
- The scoring scale gives students clear information about their work and a vocabulary for discussion.
- Students are usually less intimidated by an overall "impression" than by extensive markings or a letter grade.

Portfolios

Portfolio assessment is another popular method of evaluating student writing. Like a visual artist's portfolio, a student writer's portfolio is a representative collection of work. What is considered representative, however, varies greatly from teacher to teacher and from school to school. Sometimes *portfolio* denotes nothing more than a folder in which students keep all their work—prewriting, drafts, revisions, and finished papers—for the entire year. According to one common definition, however, a portfolio has the following distinguishing elements:

- **Choice.** Students (and sometimes teachers) select the pieces of writing they want to include. The teacher determines the types of items for the portfolios, depending on the course goals, but students decide which particular pieces to include.
- **Process.** Portfolios are not limited to finished papers. These writing collections include evidence of each student's individual writing process; this evidence may include every scrap of paper from prewriting to a complete essay as well as isolated exploratory writing or exercises. Portfolios also represent work over a period of time.
- **Self-Reflection.** Portfolios are annotated. They include students' written reflections about their writings, about their strategies as writers, and about the changes in both over time. (A portfolio may also include the teacher's written responses or student-teacher exchanges.)

Design and Management. The specific contents of writing portfolios can be adapted to the needs of a particular school or teacher. But advance planning of the contents is necessary. A portfolio system should have a table of contents that makes clear each element of the portfolio. For example, it might include

- an introduction (or afterword) in which the student discusses the whole portfolio
- two completed essays (persuasion, expressive writing, etc.), one with all working notes and drafts
- "Writer's Choice" (best or most meaningful writing), with explanation
- "Teacher's Choice," with explanation

Each student might even include his or her *least* satisfactory writing, with a rationale.

> "Students should see the portfolios first as their own personal record, resource, and achievement. Portfolios give students a sense of themselves as working writers."

While maintaining the portfolio should be each student's responsibility, the portfolio is shared with and is open to the teacher. Portfolios are a form of publishing to be used in writing groups, in displays, and with home audiences.

Assessment. Because portfolios are comprehensive yet selective, structured yet participatory, they offer a natural avenue of assessment. Many possibilities exist for you to personalize the assessment of your students' portfolios:

- Designing a portfolio with the idea that its full contents will be evaluated
- Designating certain parts for evaluation
- Assessing at specified intervals or at year-end
- Combining portfolio assessment with other forms of assessment

Exactly *how* you assess the pieces in a portfolio will vary as well. Perhaps, in cooperation with your students, you can decide which pieces will receive a grade, which a holistic score, which a simple check-off for inclusion, etc.

Even though they offer advantages for assessment, portfolios should not be tied too tightly to a grade. Students should see the portfolios first as their own personal record, resource, and achievement. Students should not just fill the portfolios but should use and learn from them.

COOPERATIVE LEARNING

More and more often, teachers are urged to have students work in pairs or groups. Collaboration not only yields higher individual achievement but also improves social skills and fosters responsibility for learning.

Yet putting cooperative learning into practice is not a simple matter of grouping students and saying, "Get to work!" Here are some ideas for creating a cooperative classroom.

Who, How Many, and for How Long?

Size. Neither research nor experience has produced absolutes about group size or formation. Generally, though, teachers who use groups recommend a minimum of four students and a maximum of six. Pairs may be useful in early work to get students accustomed to working together and in some specific activities such as proofreading; but pairs might not generate the creative sparks that groups can.

Structure. Some teachers favor a random grouping method, such as counting off, to create heterogeneous mixes. Others appoint students to groups after considering student proficiencies, diversities, and leadership. Letting students form their own groups is less common, but some teachers do so, believing that students naturally form workable ensembles.

Duration. Groups do not need to stay together for an entire term or year. However, don't reorganize them too often. Members need sufficient time to get to know each other and to contribute equally. You might use standing groups for core work and develop new configurations for special activities.

What Activities?

With time and experience, teachers often find ways to transform favorite assignments and classwork from individual to collaborative work. Here are some general suggestions.

1. **Peer Response, Revising, and Proofreading.** These are probably the most familiar cooperative activities. Getting feedback on drafts helps writers, as does proofreading the drafts of others. Actually revising together to rework the draft is another possible step.
2. **Group Prewriting and Writing.** Finding, choosing, and narrowing topics are all good collaborative projects. When you assign a research paper or a persuasive paper, for example, each student will get more ideas by listening to others. Also, give students chances to be coauthors. For example, you might start by asking pairs of students to coauthor a paragraph (you might supply the same data to the whole class). Afterward, be sure to have a discussion about the process: who did what, what the benefits and problems were, and what personal insights each student had.
3. **Learning Teams and Expert Groups.** Students can study for quizzes and tests in teams, helping each other master the material. Expert groups can research a topic and present their findings to the class or to other groups. The students learn by researching, as well as by teaching one another.
4. **Jigsawing.** Jigsawing is actually a pattern for disseminating new learning. Students break up tasks (summarizing textbook chapters, researching rhetorical techniques, etc.), and then teach each other. Simple jigsawing occurs in a single group. Group jigsawing is accomplished by forming second-level groups. Within each original group, students count off and then regroup according to their numbers. Then all "one's" form a new group, all "two's," and so on. Each student teaches the new material to the second group.

How to Manage?

Spelling Things Out. Clear instructions are important in cooperative learning, particularly in early trials. Develop written guidelines requiring students to

- keep work and comments focused on the task, not on people
- combine criticism with concrete suggestions and positive observations
- frequently paraphrase others' points and explanations

Describe the specific product (not necessarily a tangible one) expected of the group work; also list steps, tasks, and time limits. Eventually you will be able to manage the groups' activities more informally. At first, though, a written reference keeps students on track and heads off confusion or disputes.

Establishing Roles. Functional roles in groups are a recorder or reporter who takes notes and speaks for the group (two different students could serve), someone who collects needed classroom materials, and possibly a leader or manager. Let students assign these roles and suggest others.

Facilitating. During group work, the teacher must be on the periphery of the action. As a facilitator, your job is to move freely among groups to pose questions, suggest tactics, and answer legitimate questions.

Above all, have patience. A certain amount of digression as students work is all right. In the beginning, peer responses such as "I don't like this part" will be typical. As you ask questions and model responses, students' responses will become more concrete.

Evaluating. A group grade or some other form of evaluation for a collaborative project not only helps students' commitment and cohesion but also shapes their attitude toward cooperative learning. Depending on the product, you may

- give a group grade
- give a group grade plus individual grades
- create a class (audience) evaluation form for oral reports
- form panels of peer reviewers

Whatever assessment method you choose, clearly state it, along with any evaluation criteria, before work starts.

Students will probably feel anxious about grades that hinge on others' work, and that anxiety should be addressed in class. You can help students to see the positive aspects of collaboration. In their lives after school, they will be working collaboratively in their jobs. Life and work are filled with the need to cooperate with others.

INTEGRATING GRAMMAR, USAGE, AND MECHANICS WITH WRITING

An integrated language arts curriculum, in some form or another, is now familiar in schools and textbooks. Reading, writing, speaking, listening, and viewing are linked because all reinforce one another to develop literacy. In addition, more and more educators are stressing the integration of instruction in grammar, usage, and mechanics with instruction in reading and writing.

Seizing the Moment. This idea is another manifestation of the "teachable moment": Learning within a *context*—a real situation—is more relevant, more personal, and thus more lasting. For example, teaching the forms of the verb *be* is a natural spinoff when students are revising their drafts for strong verb choices.

Using Research. Research supports the integrated approach by showing that the skill-and-drills method of teaching grammar, usage, and mechanics has real limitations. Many students who pass mastery tests still can't apply the skills. But how can teachers teach differently? With increasing frequency, researchers, teachers, and textbook writers offer concrete strategies for integrating the language arts.

Lesson Ideas

Here are some general tips for developing an integrated program in which lessons in grammar, usage, and mechanics are keyed to writing assignments.

1. Match instruction to the specific writing assignment whenever possible. A cause-and-effect essay, for instance, is a good opportunity to teach adverb clauses, which express relationship.

2. Use students' drafts as a source of teaching topics. Almost any grammar instruction can be relevant to the writing lesson if the examples, whether problems or successes, come from the students' own work. Take advantage of portfolios to find fragments, overuse of passive voice, and other problem areas that the whole class can examine, discuss, and revise.

3. Reserve instruction for the revising and proofreading stages. Any nervousness about correctness should not inhibit free drafting. The skill or concept will suggest the timing. For example, an explanation of adverb clauses may clarify meaning during revision; an explanation of subject-verb agreement or capitalization can wait until the proofreading stage.

> "Students become active learners rather than passive ones. They look for errors or weaknesses, decide how to fix the problems, and try new syntactic effects."

4. Move from identification to participation to instruction. One good pattern for teaching is to

- identify briefly, with some examples, the topic or element (punctuation of dialogue; dangling modifiers)
- have students find and discuss instances of that topic or element in their papers
- present a fuller lesson on the topic or element, moving directly to students' revising or proofreading

5. Have students keep personal checklists for editing. As students uncover their own problem areas or learn new skills that they want to retain, they can build individual final checklists to use with subsequent papers. A few possibilities for topics keyed to types of writing are

- **Cause and effect:** adverb clauses; subordinating conjunctions and conjunctive adverbs
- **Cause and effect; problem solving:** the *affect-effect* distinction; parallelism
- **Comparison and contrast:** degrees of comparison

- **Narratives:** active voice and passive voice; pronoun case; pronoun reference
- **Process explanations:** colons; items in a series
- **Writing about literature; research reports:** punctuating quotations; incorporating quotations into sentences
- **Writing about literature; reviews:** the *allusion-illusion* distinction; punctuating titles of works; present (historical/literary) tense versus past tense
- **Creative writing:** punctuating dialogue; fragments
- **Journalistic reporting:** appositives; proper nouns and adjectives
- **Description:** parts of speech—adjectives, adverbs, verbs, nouns

Appeal and Advantages

While no new pedagogy will make every student love infinitives, integrating grammar with students' own writing will make the instruction far more interesting than will out-of-context drills. The advantages for students' achievement are numerous.

Rather than learning a string of concepts to be applied later, students deal with problems as they occur and with skills when they are needed. Students recognize—in a year-long continuum of learning—that grammar, usage, and mechanics are useful and necessary to the meaning of writing.

Students become active learners rather than passive ones. They look for errors or weaknesses, decide how to fix the problems, and try new syntactic effects. Students become critical thinkers by applying evaluative criteria to their own writing.

MULTICULTURALISM

The United States is becoming increasingly diverse, both ethnically and culturally. In fact, the Census Bureau projects that by the year 2050, non-Hispanic whites will make up about 53 percent of the U.S. population. Hispanics will comprise 23 percent, African Americans 16 percent, Asian Americans 10 percent, and American Indians slightly more than 1 percent.

As educators, we know the importance of preparing our students to live in our changing society. We want our students to understand and take pride in their own unique ethnic and cultural heritage. We also want them to appreciate the shared cultural heritage of the United States.

To help you meet the needs of students in a multicultural society, *English Workshop* provides culturally diverse topics in assignments, exercises, examples, and models. It is our hope that such topics will provide support for your efforts to build your students' self-esteem and to foster a sense of community in your classroom and our society.

1866

ENGLISH WORKSHOP—FIRST COURSE
ANSWER KEY: Pupil's Edition

CHAPTER 1: THE WRITING PROCESS

PREWRITING: JOURNALS AND FREEWRITING
EXERCISE 1, page 1
(Answers will vary. All responses should be based on the broad subject of a personal experience or event that made the writer proud or happy. Commend work that shows an attempt to let ideas flow freely. Do not base your evaluation of the student's work on spelling, mechanics, or form.)

PREWRITING: BRAINSTORMING AND CLUSTERING
EXERCISE 2, page 2
(Answers will vary. Commend partners who work well together and who listen to and consider each other's ideas. Encourage partners to examine each other's work. Point out that brainstorming can be especially effective as an idea-gathering tool because it allows people to learn from others' points of view. Do not base your evaluation of the student's work on spelling, mechanics, or form. Stress that prewriting is a creative, thought-generating time and that students will have several chances at further stages in the writing process to correct errors and to refine their sentences.)

PREWRITING: ASKING QUESTIONS
EXERCISE 3, page 3
(Answers will vary. Possible responses are given. Commend work that shows evidence of effective use of the 5W–How? questions to explore a subject thoroughly.)

Who went to the class picnic?
What kind of food was served?
Where was the picnic held?
When did the picnic end?
Why did so few people go to the picnic?
How was the food kept fresh?

EXERCISE 4, page 4
(Answers will vary. Possible responses are given. Commend work that shows imagination and effective use of "What if?" questions. Commend partners who work well together.)

What if the crying of the word processor disturbs the neighbors?
What if the word processor stops crying when you key in a happy poem?

PREWRITING: ARRANGING IDEAS
EXERCISE 5, page 5
(Answers will vary. Possible responses are given.)
1. chronological; importance; logical
2. spatial; importance
3. logical; spatial
4. importance

WRITING A FIRST DRAFT
EXERCISE 6, page 6
(Answers will vary. The description will be satisfactory if the student lists details in spatial order—e.g., from left to right or from front to back. The draft description should include enough details to leave the reader with a clear picture of the place.)

EVALUATING
EXERCISE 7, page 8
(Answers will vary. Possible responses are given. Commend work that relies on the evaluation standards and the tips for peer evaluation and that is clearly intended to be helpful and constructive.)

1. I like the tone of this paragraph. The details helped me to understand why the park is a peaceful place where you can go and think.
2. Perhaps you could shorten the first sentence. Do you think that the phrases "to think" and "just get my thoughts together" say the same thing? Maybe you could take one of those phrases out.
3. Maybe you could add some information. How about saying, "It was named for Benjamin Banneker, who was an African American astronomer"?
4. I'd think about switching the order of the third and fourth sentences to keep the information about Benjamin Banneker together.
5. I think that more details might help the last sentence. For example, you might change "the birds" to "the chirping birds." I think that change would help the reader hear the sounds more clearly.

REVISING
EXERCISE 8, page 9
(Answers will vary. Students will probably need to use the revision techniques from the chart to improve their drafts at least two or three times.)

PROOFREADING AND PUBLISHING
EXERCISE 9, page 10
1. commas to set off *who was born in Russia*; *their* should be *there*
2. *union* should be *Union*; *brung* should be *brought*; *intresting* should be *interesting*
3. *anothr* should be *another*
4. delete the first comma; insert *a* before *smaller*; *there was* should be *there were*
5. add a period to end the last sentence

EXERCISE 10, page 12
(Answers will vary. Responses should be focused and concrete. Commend ideas that show creative thinking.)

9

EXERCISE 11, page 12

(Answers will vary. Final drafts should be free of errors in spelling, grammar, usage, and mechanics. Drafts should follow the Guidelines for Manuscript Form on page 11.)

CHAPTER 2: PARAGRAPH WORKSHOPS

MAIN IDEAS AND TOPIC SENTENCES
EXERCISE 1, page 13

1. Main Idea: Pilar is talented.
   Topic Sentence: Pilar is definitely a person of many talents.
2. Main Idea: Little by little, Salim was able to climb the rope toward the top of the gymnasium.
   Topic Sentence: none
3. Main Idea: A number of foods originated in the Americas.
   Topic Sentence: Many important food crops were first grown in the Americas.
4. Main Idea: Some Spanish names for girls are Spanish words as well.
   Topic Sentence: Many Spanish girls have names that are also words in the Spanish language.

UNITY AND COHERENCE
EXERCISE 2, page 15

1. At a museum I saw a chess set that had castles shaped like real fortresses.
2. The city's parks and museums are also exceptional.

EXERCISE 3, page 16

With a few simple steps, you can make a healthful, nutritious omelet. <u>First</u>, chop some vegetables, such as green peppers and onions. <u>Next</u>, separate the whites from the yolks of three eggs. Place the whites in a medium-sized bowl, <u>and</u> whip them. <u>Then</u> pour the egg whites into a pan coated with a little olive oil. Allow them to cook for a minute or two. <u>Finally</u>, add your chopped vegetables, <u>and</u> fold half of the egg-white mixture over them. Cook the omelet thoroughly.

USING DESCRIPTION AND NARRATION
EXERCISE 4, page 17

(Answers will vary. This exercise will be satisfactorily completed if the students list sensory details in spatial order—from far away to near, from left to right, or from top to bottom. There should be enough sensory details to leave the reader with a clear picture of the subject described.)

EXERCISE 5, page 18

(Answers will vary. Each of the student's chronological lists should contain four or more events in the story and four or more steps in the process.)

USING COMPARISON/CONTRAST AND EVALUATION
EXERCISE 6, page 19

(Answers will vary. This exercise will be satisfactorily completed if the student identifies at least three similarities and at least three differences.)

EXERCISE 7, page 20

(Answers will vary but are considered acceptable if they follow the example's structure: state an opinion, and offer at least two reasons supporting that opinion.)

CHAPTER 3: COMPOSITION WORKSHOPS

PLANNING A COMPOSITION
EXERCISE 1, page 21

(Answers will vary. Possible responses are given.)

CAUSES OF FOREST FIRES
   people—cause 90 percent of all forest fires
   people carelessly flipping lighted matches into wooded areas
   smoldering campfires left by campers
   some fires deliberately set
   lightning, another cause of fire

EFFECTS ON WILDLIFE
   loss of many birds' and animals' lives in fire
   lack of food, wildlife die
   fish poisoned by streams clogged with ashes

WAYS TO LIMIT FOREST FIRE DAMAGE
   teach people to appreciate the value of their forests
   could increase the number of lookout towers
   train more firefighters

EXERCISE 2, page 22

(Answers will vary. Possible responses are given.)

   I. Causes of forest fires
      A. People
         1. Carelessly flip lighted matches into wooded areas
         2. Leave campfires smoldering
         3. Deliberately set fires
      B. Lightning
   II. Effects on wildlife
      A. Deaths from fire and smoke
      B. Deaths from lack of food
      C. Deaths from poisoning by streams clogged with ashes
   III. Ways to limit forest fire damage
      A. Teaching people to appreciate the value of their forests
      B. Increasing the number of lookout towers
      C. Training more firefighters

WRITING INTRODUCTIONS
EXERCISE 3, page 24

1. State an interesting or startling fact
2. Ask a question
3. State an interesting or startling fact
4. Tell an anecdote

WRITING CONCLUSIONS
EXERCISE 4, page 26

(Answers will vary, but students' conclusions should tie together the ideas in the composition by referring to the main idea. The conclusions should give the feeling of completion.)

CHAPTER 4:
EXPRESSING YOURSELF

A JOURNAL ENTRY
THINKING ABOUT THE MODEL, page 27
1. All five kinds of details appear in the journal entry: people (writer and her friends); places (lake); events (moving, activities at the lake); thoughts and feelings (about move, lake, missing friends).
2. The writer is sad about leaving. *feel the cool breeze* (touch); *rippled the water* (sight); *oak leaves rattle* (hearing)

ASSIGNMENT: WRITING A JOURNAL ENTRY, page 28
TO THE TEACHER: An evaluation scale is not appropriate for a journal entry. You can give credit for completion of the assignment.

A CHILDHOOD MEMORY
THINKING ABOUT THE MODEL, page 31
1. The first sentence—"You can't break the law of gravity"—followed by mention of the sled, tells the reader something interesting is probably about to happen.
2. The old sled, given by the grandparents, belonged to the writer's father. The writer imagined that sledding would be easy. The reader understands that the writer's fearlessness probably led to the fall.
3. eyes squinted against the cold; The snow crunched; butterflies in my stomach; wind was so cold I couldn't breathe; I felt…weightless.
4. the detailed memory of the sled; the writer's excitement in describing the ride down the hill; the writer stating that a lesson was learned.

ASSIGNMENT: WRITING ABOUT A CHILDHOOD MEMORY, page 33
TO THE TEACHER: The following is a grading scale you may wish to use in evaluating students' narratives.

SCORE POINT 4
4 = These narratives have interesting beginnings.
These narratives contain helpful background information.
Events are arranged appropriately.
Details about sights, sounds, smells, tastes, and textures are used effectively.
These narratives have effective endings.

SCORE POINT 3
3 = These narratives have fairly interesting beginnings.
These narratives contain fairly helpful background information.
Events are arranged fairly appropriately.
Details about sights, sounds, smells, tastes, and textures are used fairly effectively.
These narratives have fairly effective endings.

SCORE POINT 2
2 = These narratives do not necessarily have interesting beginnings.
These narratives do not necessarily contain helpful background information.
Events are not necessarily arranged appropriately.
Details about sights, sounds, smells, tastes, and textures are not necessarily used effectively.
These narratives do not necessarily have effective endings.

SCORE POINT 1
1 = These narratives do not have interesting beginnings.
These narratives do not contain helpful background information.
Events are not arranged appropriately.
Details about sights, sounds, smells, tastes, and textures are not used effectively.
These narratives do not have effective endings.

CHAPTER 5:
CREATIVE WRITING

A TALL TALE
THINKING ABOUT THE MODEL, page 41
1. first words she spoke, counting all grains of rice in pantry, counting cars on freeway, family wearing earmuffs, flying fingers creating a whirlwind, Miriam's shopping ability, traffic jam from New Mexico to New Hampshire, tying up all telephone lines in country, Prime Minister calling, helping President with taxes, hurricanes and tornadoes, reaching West Coast before leaving East Coast, blowing snow off Mount Everest and creating oasis in the Sahara
2. the whirlwinds, the tornadoes and hurricanes, being featured on national news, being asked for advice by the Prime Minister and the President, being a math genius as well as an extraordinary athlete
3. *problems created*: noise in parents' house, whirlwind, traffic jam, tied up telephone lines, hurricanes and tornadoes
problems solved: cost of groceries, cost of wall around Great Britain, getting rid of national debt
4. contractions such as *that's, what's,* and *didn't*; quick as a flash; Next thing they knew; showed up on Miriam's street; took up; They say; Last I heard
5. run from the West Coast to the East Coast *or* run up Mount Everest

ASSIGNMENT: WRITING A TALL TALE, page 42
TO THE TEACHER: The following is a grading scale you may wish to use in evaluating students' tales.

SCORE POINT 4
4 = The tale has a beginning that effectively grabs the reader's interest.
The tale is humorous and includes effective exaggeration and unlikely events.
The tale includes effective details of the characters' appearance and behavior.

11

The tale effectively uses informal and colorful language.

The tale describes events in chronological order.

The tale has an ending that satisfies the reader's curiosity.

SCORE POINT 3

3 = The tale has a beginning that fairly effectively grabs the reader's interest.

The tale is humorous and includes fairly effective exaggeration and unlikely events.

The tale includes fairly effective details of the characters' appearance and behavior.

The tale fairly effectively uses informal and colorful language.

The tale describes events in a fairly effective order.

The tale has an ending that is fairly effective

SCORE POINT 2

2 = The tale has a beginning that does not necessarily grab the reader's interest.

The tale is not necessarily humorous and may not include exaggeration and unlikely events.

The tale may include details of the characters' appearance and behavior, but they may not be effective.

The tale may use informal and colorful language, but not effectively.

The tale describes events in an order that is somewhat tied together.

The tale has an ending that is not necessarily effective.

SCORE POINT 1

1 = The tale does not have a beginning that grabs the reader's interest.

The tale is not humorous and includes little, if any, exaggeration and few, if any, unlikely events.

The tale includes few, if any, details of the characters' appearance and behavior.

The tale does not use informal or colorful language effectively.

The tale does not describe events in any order.

The tale does not have an effective, satisfying ending.

CHAPTER 6: INFORMING OTHERS

A SLIDE REPORT

THINKING ABOUT THE MODEL, page 51

1. early Native North American houses
2. weather often cold and wet; cattails grew near rivers; Chippewas used young trees called saplings to build their houses; put saplings in ground and bent them together; arched saplings at top to make a dome; covered frame with tree bark or woven cattails
3. that Native Americans built houses that were right for the ways they lived and the places where they lived
4. Slide 3: shows the palmetto used by Seminoles (topic) to make a thatched roof (main idea). Slide 5: shows tipi built by Plains nations (topic) for their lives as hunters of buffalo (main idea). Slide 7: shows wickiup built by western nations such as Paiute and Nez Perce (topic) from simple materials available to them (main idea).

ASSIGNMENT: WRITING A SLIDE REPORT, page 52
TO THE TEACHER: The following is a grading scale you may wish to use in evaluating student's slide report.

SCORE POINT 4

4 = The report is based on a sufficiently narrow topic.

The report includes enough facts to make the report clear and interesting.

The report has a clear main idea.

The report includes slides that each show something about the topic and the main idea.

The report presents facts and details in an order that makes sense.

SCORE POINT 3

3 = The report is based on a fairly narrow topic.

The report includes mostly adequate facts to make the report clear and interesting.

The report has a fairly clear main idea.

The report includes slides most of which show something about the topic and the main idea.

The report presents most facts and details in an order that makes sense.

SCORE POINT 2

2 = The report is not necessarily based on a narrow topic.

The report includes some facts but not necessarily enough to make the report clear and interesting.

The report does not necessarily have a clear main idea.

The report includes slides some of which show something about the topic and the main idea.

The report presents some facts and details in an order that makes sense, but some facts and details are misplaced.

SCORE POINT 1

1 = The report is not based on a narrow topic.

The report does not include enough facts to make the report clear and interesting.

The report does not have a clear main idea.

The report includes few, if any, slides that show something about the topic and the main idea.

The report presents facts and details in an order that does not make sense.

CHAPTER 7: PERSUADING OTHERS

A LETTER TO THE EDITOR
THINKING ABOUT THE MODEL, page 60
(Answers will vary. Possible responses are given.)
1. that the parent-teacher organization should vote to spend its money on repairing the school's basketball court
2. A repaired court would result in greater safety for students.
3. that the parent-teacher organization has just completed its yearly fund drive; that weeds have grown up between cracks; that the principal has closed the court; that more than one hundred students tried out for the basketball team last year; that the school does not have a playground; that students sometimes play on sidewalks or in streets
4. *safe* place; *crowded* sidewalks
5. that a better court would result in greater safety for students; last
6. the last sentence in the letter

ASSIGNMENT: WRITING A LETTER TO THE EDITOR, page 61
TO THE TEACHER: The following is a grading scale you may wish to use in evaluating students' letters.

SCORE POINT 4
4 = The letter clearly states an opinion.
The letter has the necessary support for the opinion, including reasons, facts, and words that affect readers' emotions.
The letter uses order of importance effectively.
The letter ends with a restatement of the opinion.

SCORE POINT 3
3 = The letter states an opinion in a fairly clear manner.
The letter includes fairly effective support for the opinion, including reasons, facts, and words that affect readers' emotions.
The letter uses order of importance in a fairly effective way.
The letter ends with a fairly clear restatement of the opinion.

SCORE POINT 2
2 = The letter states an opinion in a manner that is not clear.
The letter includes at least some support for the opinion, including reasons, facts, and words that affect readers' feelings.
The letter may use order of importance, but not effectively.
The letter ends with a restatement that is not clear.

SCORE POINT 1
1 = The letter does not clearly state an opinion.
The letter provides little support, if any, for whatever opinion is suggested.
The letter does not use order of importance.
The letter does not end with a restatement of the suggested opinion.

CHAPTER 8: SENTENCE WORKSHOPS

SENTENCE FRAGMENTS
EXERCISE 1, page 69
1. sent.
2. frag.
3. sent.
4. sent.
5. frag.
6. sent.
7. frag.
8. frag.
9. sent.
10. frag.

EXERCISE 2, page 70
(Answers may vary. Possible responses are given.)
1. The students worked all night long on the decorations for the dance.
2. While we were visiting the state of Texas, we saw the Alamo.
3. My sister loves the musical group known as 10,000 Maniacs.
4. In the distance, the tall pine trees created a sharp contrast to the aspens.
5. The artist's tools include a palette knife, an easel, some paints, brushes, and a canvas.

RUN-ON SENTENCES
EXERCISE 3, page 72
(Answers may vary. Possible responses are given.)
1. The farm is in Pennsylvania. It is near the city of Gettysburg.
2. Garulo went to Argentina. He learned about Falabella horses there.
3. They look just like full-sized horses, but they are the size of dogs.
4. They are very tame, and they seem to enjoy performing.
5. Visitors can watch the miniature horses jump. These animals also dance and pull tiny wagons.

EXERCISE 4, page 72
(Answers may vary. Possible responses are given.)

Our class went on a spring trip to Baltimore, Maryland. It was really fun. In the morning, we strolled along the Inner Harbor and looked at all the sailboats. We saw a tropical rain forest and a coral reef at the National Aquarium in Baltimore. Later we visited Fort McHenry. The flag waving over this fort gave Francis Scott Key the idea to write "The Star-Spangled Banner." Finally, we toured the USS *Constellation*, one of the first U.S. warships. It was built in 1797.

COMBINING BY INSERTING WORDS AND PHRASES
EXERCISE 5, page 73
1. The spider has eight long legs.
2. The painting shows boats sailing on the sea.
3. Pat the dog gently.
4. May I have some broiled fish?
5. Poison ivy grows with clusters of three leaves.

EXERCISE 6, page 74
1. As he grew up in the colony of New York, he became friendly with the Iroquois, a Native American group living nearby.
2. During the winter of 1712–1713, he lived as the adopted son of Quayhant, an Iroquois leader.

13

3. Over the years, Weiser became a close friend of Shikellamy, one of the Iroquois.
4. In 1729 Conrad Weiser and his wife and children moved to Pennsylvania.
5. They settled with other German immigrants at the foot of Eagle Peak.
6. Weiser, a farmer and a tanner, owned eight hundred acres of land.
7. He and his family lived in a one-room, German-style house with an attic.
8. Weiser added a room to the house in 1751.
9. Later Weiser worked with James Logan, the Provincial Secretary of Pennsylvania.
10. Both Shikellamy and Weiser were helpful to Logan in keeping peace with the Iroquois.

COMBINING BY USING CONNECTING WORDS
EXERCISE 7, page 75
1. Juan and Susanna are absent today.
2. I enjoy mountain hikes, but this mountain is too steep.
3. George Winston writes songs and plays the piano.
4. Could you leave my book on the table or put it on my desk?
5. Did you go to the game alone, or were you with a group?

EXERCISE 8, page 76
1. The woodchuck is a mammal that belongs to the squirrel family.
2. Some people who live in Canada and the United States call woodchucks by their other name, "groundhogs."
3. Woodchucks enjoy alfalfa and clover, which are wild plants.
4. Woodchucks eat large amounts of food before they hibernate in the winter.
5. Robert Frost wrote an interesting poem that is called "A Drumlin Woodchuck."

IMPROVING SENTENCE STYLE
EXERCISE 9, page 78
(Answers may vary. Possible responses are given.)
1. Susannah Wheatley, who lived in Boston, was the wife of a wealthy merchant. She bought a young African woman as a slave and named the woman Phillis Wheatley.
2. Phillis worked in the Wheatley household, but she also learned how to speak, read, and write English. In addition, she studied Latin and began to write poetry.
3. She read her poems to Susannah Wheatley, who enjoyed them. Susannah took Phillis to friends' homes so Phillis could read her poems to these friends.
4. There was trouble in the colonies, and British soldiers arrived in Boston in 1768. Phillis wrote a poem called "On the Arrival of the Ships of War, and Landing of the Troops."
5. In 1772, Phillis went to England because Susannah had arranged for a London publisher to print a book of Phillis's poems. Phillis went to England, where many people hailed her as a great poet.

EXERCISE 10, page 78
(Answers may vary. Possible responses are given.)
1. We spent many days rehearsing the play *Our Town*.
2. Many people in my neighborhood work hard to keep the sidewalks free of litter.
3. I am very happy to play on a winning soccer team.
4. If it rains, the graduation ceremony will be in the gym.
5. My two pets are Chips, a dog, and Mimi, a cat.

CHAPTER REVIEW
A., p. 79
(Answers may vary. Possible responses are given.)

Toronto is the second largest city in Canada, after Montreal. Toronto is one of Canada's major ports, and ships arrive there from all over the world. It is also a bustling commercial center. Manufactured goods include machinery, electrical appliances, and clothing. Many of these products are exported to foreign countries. Twice in Canada's history Toronto was the nation's capital. The first time was from 1849 to 1851, and the second time was from 1855 to 1859.

B., p. 79
(Answers may vary. Possible responses are given.)

I know the manager of the arboretum. He is a friendly man named Frank Alonzo. He enjoys taking people on tours through the arboretum. I have hiked through the arboretum with him many times. I always stop at my favorite tree, a pink dogwood. It is not really rare, but it is especially beautiful in late spring, when it is covered with pink blossoms. This spring the dogwood surprised me with something new. It had a fragile nest on one of its lower branches. When I stood on tiptoe, I could see a baby bird in the nest. The baby bird will leave the nest by late summer. Mr. Alonzo said that when he takes the nest down in the fall, he will give it to me.

C., p. 80
(Answers may vary. Possible responses are given.)

When my grandmother was twenty-one, her grandfather gave her a special present. Her grandfather, my great-great-grandfather, was a carpenter. One morning in 1914, he was building a fence for someone when a storm came up suddenly. Lightning hit a tree, and a huge branch fell to the ground. As he hurried into a shed to get out of the rain, he saw something strange in the huge branch. After the storm, he examined the branch and found a beautiful knot in it. With his saw, he cut the big knot out of the branch and took the knot home. He carved out the wood all around the knot and made a beautiful bowl, which he gave to my grandmother for her birthday. Many years later, my grandmother gave the bowl to my mother. Someday my mother will give it to me. Every time I examine the beautiful, smooth wood, I think of my great-great-grandfather. I think that **he was a** great artist, and I wish that I had known him.

CHAPTER 9: LANGUAGE WORKSHOPS

CHOOSING YOUR WORDS I
EXERCISE 1, page 81
(Answers will vary. Possible responses are given.)
1. The children decided to end their argument and apologize to each other.
2. Ariel feared we would be late and asked us to hurry.
3. Our group met during study hall and discussed a few ideas.
4. Each day after school, I must complete my homework before I am allowed to watch television.
5. Their soccer team was much stronger than ours, and they beat us soundly.
6. The first story is boring, but the next one is worth reading.
7. Saturday is an active day, but on Sundays I usually stay at home all afternoon.
8. The investigator followed Jules for an hour, but later Jules slipped away and vanished.
9. Mrs. Wong acted differently after she had heard the reason for the noise.
10. That driver likes sports sedans but is truly impressed by roadsters.

EXERCISE 2, page 82
(Answers will vary. Possible responses given.)
1. odor–Odor creates a more unpleasant sensory image than smell.
2. rumor–A rumor is less reliable than a report.
3. fight–A fight sounds less reasonable than a disagreement.
4. habit–A habit creates the impression that the behavior is automatic rather than thoughtful.
5. skinny–Skinny implies that someone is too slim, almost unhealthy.

CHOOSING YOUR WORDS II
EXERCISE 3, page 83
(Answers will vary. Possible responses are given.)
1. That dog of yours is larger than any other I've seen.
2. Baseball practice made me incredibly hungry.
3. When Elise heard the noise, she turned pale.
4. I want you to run as fast as you can when you hear the starting gun.
5. The hero was a quiet, thoughtful man.

EXERCISE 4, page 84
(Answers will vary. Possible responses are given.)
1. The photo had to be trimmed so it wouldn't extend into the area where the pages meet in the book.
2. The banker reinvested the funds before the contract ended and payment had to be made.
3. Enter the front of the boat from the left side.
4. The defensive back who plays in front of the goalkeeper sent the ball up the field by hitting it with her head.
5. Should I play the short musical passage fast?

CHAPTER REVIEW
A., page 85
(Answers will vary. Possible responses are given.)
[1] An elephant is odd in certain ways. [2] For one thing, it is a very large animal! [3] An elephant can weigh many thousands of pounds. [4] Also, it has a fascinating trunk. [5] An elephant uses its trunk in many ways. [6] It smells with it, picks up food with it, and drinks with it. [7] Elephants drink a lot. [8] An elephant can drink up to twenty gallons of water per day. [9] Baby elephant are cute animals. [10] Today I had a great idea to go to the circus.

B., page 86
1. chalky
2. gloomy
3. dull
4. sour
5. smirk

C., page 86
(Answers will vary. Possible responses are given.)
1. When the music stopped, Ed stood there and looked uncertain.
2. You'll like Donna because she has such a good sense of humor.
3. The mattress that I slept on last night was too firm for my taste.
4. When I stood up to speak, I felt nervous and faint.

D., page 86
(Answers will vary. Possible responses are given.)
<u>Hair Styles</u>
1. frost—Frost your bangs a different color. (lighten selected strands of hair)
2. mohawk—Alan wore a mohawk to school. (hair from the forehead to the back of the head and shaved on both sides)
3. French braid—Sukie put her hair in a French braid. (style of braiding)
4. spiked hair—The band members wore spiked hair. (hair that has been stiffened with gel and made to stand straight up)
5. buzz cut—Does your uncle have a buzz cut? (hair that is shaved all the way around, like an Army haircut)

CHAPTER 10: THE SENTENCE

SENTENCE SENSE
EXERCISE 1, page 88
1. n.s.
2. s.; ?
3. n.s.
4. s.; . *or* !
5. s.; .
6. s.; .
7. n.s.
8. s.; .
9. s.; . *or* !
10. s.; ?

EXERCISE 2, page 88
1. dec.; .
2. exc.; !
3. imp.; . *or* !
4. exc.; ! *or* dec.; .
5. int.; ?

THE SUBJECT
EXERCISE 3, page 89
1. scientists
2. United States National Cancer Institute
3. Jenna
4. rain forest
5. "El Yunque"
6. Hurricane Hugo
7. birds
8. cassowaries
9. cassowary
10. people

EXERCISE 4, page 90
1. The <u>people</u> of this culture
2. The <u>buildings</u> of their capital city
3. The <u>capital</u>, called Great Zimbabwe,
4. More than ten thousand <u>people</u>
5. fascinated <u>tourists</u>

THE PREDICATE
EXERCISE 5, page 91
1. gathered along the shore of New York Harbor
2. was the hundredth birthday of Lady Liberty
3. For the big event, repaired the statue
4. cost more than sixty-nine million dollars
5. was ready for her birthday party
6. had new elevators, a new torch, and a repaired crown
7. At the celebration, saw a dazzling display of fireworks
8. soared into the sky over the harbor
9. From the enormous crowd of people came
10. was one of the largest displays of fireworks in the history of the United States

EXERCISE 6, page 92
1. <u>writes</u> funny stories about his childhood
2. <u>will be closed</u> on Fridays during the summer
3. <u>want</u> pizza and salad for supper
4. <u>can</u> never <u>remember</u> our new telephone number
5. <u>Put</u> the dirty dishes in the sink

COMPOUND SUBJECTS AND COMPOUND VERBS
EXERCISE 7, page 93
S.	V.
1. Apples; oranges	are
2. Vitamin C; fiber	are found
3. oranges; juice	contain
4. Iron; vitamins	are
5. eggs; eggs	are

EXERCISE 8, page 94
S.	V.
1. sun	gives; provides
2. penguins	stand; cuddle
3. John	bought; arrived
4. birds; dinosaurs	existed; are
5. leaves	turn; fall
6. (you)	Staple; clip
7. *Titanic*	hit; sank
8. problems	look; were
9. Father	Will drive; (will) take
10. Magda	read; wrote

CHAPTER REVIEW
A., page 95
1. imp.; .
2. exc.; !
3. int.; ?
4. dec.; .
5. imp.; . *or* !

B., page 95
1. <u>The baseball team</u> <u>had never won a championship in the history of our school.</u>
2. During the season, <u>the players and coaches</u> <u>worked hard.</u>
3. <u>Their dedication to the game</u> <u>was obvious.</u>
4. Among their greatest achievements was <u>perfect attendance by each player.</u>
5. <u>People in this town</u> <u>may never again feel such pride and joy.</u>

C., page 95
S.	V.
1. woman	wrote
2. she	visited
3. jail	housed
4. schoolteacher	was horrified
5. states	built

D., page 96
(Answers will vary. This exercise will be satisfactorily completed if the student's sentences include at least five compound subjects and five compound verbs labeled correctly.)

CHAPTER 11: PARTS OF SPEECH

NOUNS
EXERCISE 1, page 98
CLASS	NOUNS
1. abs.; abs.; con.	joy; time; beach
2. con.; con.	Milky Way; stars
3. con.; abs.	Harriet; eternity
4. con.; con.; con.	Thomas Edison; pioneers; movies
5. con.; con.; con.	Greece; athletes; crown

EXERCISE 2, page 98
(Answers will vary. Possible responses are given.)
1. President Clinton traveled to Little Rock, Arkansas.
2. *Coastal Waters* was written by Christine Cummins.
3. "Our Tallest Old Building," about the Empire State Building, was in *USA Today*.
4. Emma Thompson stars in *Much Ado About Nothing*.
5. Vinny moved to Salzburg, Austria.

PRONOUNS
EXERCISE 3, page 99
PRON.	ANTE.
1. its, its	pony
2. his	Mr. Chisholm
3. they	flowers
4. he, his	lumberjack

5. I — Rafael
6. I — Jaime
7. his — Grandfather
8. you, your, you — Adam
9. you, me — Alejandro, Jason
10. I, he, his — *none*; Andrés

EXERCISE 4, page 100

1. Leonardo da Vinci painted his masterpiece the *Mona Lisa* in the early 1500s.
2. Some people disagree about the real name of the painting *Mona Lisa*—it could be *La Gioconda*.
3. Lisa del Giocondo was the model for the painting, and she had no eyebrows.
4. Because Mona Lisa's smile is unusual, it has caused many arguments.
5. Because many painters wanted to paint like da Vinci, they copied his masterpiece.

ADJECTIVES
EXERCISE 5, page 102

ADJ.	WORD MODIFIED
1. Most, hot, humid	tornadoes, days
2. shiny, new, old, historical	skyscrapers, buildings
3. Summer, two	temperatures, months
4. many, clear	stars, sky
5. eighty-one billion	tons

EXERCISE 6, page 102
(Answers will vary. Possible responses are given.)

1. The dress was made of taffeta and lace.
   She chose silk dress material.
2. Please stack the wood in the corner.
   I think a wood fire is more beautiful than a coal fire.
3. His committee voted on the issue.
   Too many committee members were absent.
4. Our boat comes out of the water on the day after Labor Day.
   There is a long lineup at the boat ramp.
5. Lincoln was the sixteenth president of the United States.
   Lincoln pennies are becoming more and more rare these days.
6. The scratch on my arm is from our new kitten.
   I wrote a rough draft of the letter on scratch paper.
7. The black in the painting really shows up.
   Black ink spilled on my desk.
8. My grandfather lived in Texas when he was young.
   The restaurant served my favorite Texas chili.
9. We enjoyed fresh seafood at a restaurant in Gloucester, MA.
   Seafood salad makes a tasty lunch on a warm summer day.
10. The local police chief gave an interesting speech at our school.
    My sister read a speech book before running for class president.
11. My cat knocked a glass vase off the table.
    Cat food was on sale at the supermarket.
12. Jamila likes to keep at least one flower on her windowsill.
    Do you like the flower arrangement?

DEMONSTRATIVE AND PROPER ADJECTIVES
EXERCISE 7, page 103

ADJ.	PRON.
1. this	
2. That	
3. this	
4. this	Those
5. These	

EXERCISE 8, page 104

COMMON	PROPER
1. cotton, work	
2.	French
3. immigrant	
4. heavy, gold, their, hard	
5. many, his, heavy-duty	
6. few, this, canvas, softer	
7. copper, pocket	Russian Jewish
8. blue	
9. famous	San Francisco
10. these, practical, popular, fashion	

CHAPTER REVIEW
A., page 105

1. n.; adj.
2. pron.; pron.
3. pron.; n.
4. n.; adj.
5. adj.; adj.
6. n.; n.
7. adj.; n.
8. n.; adj.
9. pron.; adj.
10. pron.; n.

B., page 105

PRON.	ANTE.
1. you	Mr. Mayor
2. his	Louis Armstrong
3. we	people
4. she, her	Wenona
5. I, my	boy

C., page 106

1. One (book)
   excellent (book)
   popular (series)
   television (series)
2. powerful (stories)
   beautiful (Yorkshire, England)
   grassy (hills)
   rich (background)
   several (characters)
   memorable (characters)
3. all (characters)
   major (characters)
4. real-life (veterinarian)
   these (stories)
   outstanding (stories)
5. many (ways)
   unforgettable (tours)
   small (towns)
   rural (towns)
   northern (part)

D., page 106
(Answers will vary. The exercise will be satisfactorily completed if the student writes five short sentences with sensory detail. Nouns, pronouns, and adjectives should be identified.)

CHAPTER 12: PARTS OF SPEECH

VERBS

EXERCISE 1, page 107
1. visited
2. Throw
3. saw
4. waters
5. melt

EXERCISE 2, page 108
1. intr.
2. trans.
3. trans.
4. trans.
5. intr.

EXERCISE 3, page 108
(Answers will vary. Possible responses are given.)
1. Did you bake <u>cookies</u> for the conference? (transitive)
   My dad bakes every Saturday. (intransitive)
2. In all the confusion, I forgot the <u>package</u>. (transitive)
   In all the confusion, I forgot. (intransitive)
3. A few in the class joined the debating <u>team</u>. (transitive)
   Everyone joined in the song. (intransitive)
4. On the weekends, my brother and I play <u>chess</u>. (transitive)
   The football team will play on Saturday. (intransitive)
5. Stop that <u>car</u>! (transitive)
   Did the car stop at the red light? (intransitive)

LINKING VERBS

EXERCISE 4, page 110
1. Is
2. appeared
3. felt
4. became
5. grew
6. seems
7. is
8. had been
9. looks
10. can be

EXERCISE 5, page 110

LINKING VERB	WORDS CONNECTED
1. appears	planet—red
2. is	It—smaller
3. has been	Mars—source
4. remains	icecap—frozen
5. grows	icecap—larger

HELPING VERBS

EXERCISE 6, page 111

VERB PHRASE	HELPING VERB
1. can be traced	can be
2. have remained	have
3. has changed	has
4. would hit	would
5. was filled	was
6. were used	were
7. had been invented	had been
8. do use	do
9. are made	are
10. have been tried	have been

EXERCISE 7, page 112

VERB PHRASE	HELPING VERB
1. had moved	had
2. had become	had
3. had been elected	had been
4. was elected	was
5. is regarded	is
6. was born	was
7. did receive	did
8. was married	was
9. had chosen	had
10. would become	would

ADVERBS

EXERCISE 8, page 114

ADVERB(S)	WORD(S) MODIFIED
1. too, too	long, expensive
2. then	Was shining
3. soon	will call
4. Suddenly, extremely	pounded, high
5. Yesterday	visited
6. fiercely, angrily	growled
7. later, unusually	seemed, heavy
8. seldom, outside	goes
9. always	does
10. well, amazingly	works, well

EXERCISE 9, page 114
(Answers will vary. Possible responses are given. Students should use a different adverb for each sentence.)
1. This puppet is quite clever.
2. Children can be surprisingly dishonest.
3. The actors were unbelievably happy after the movie reviews came out.
4. The paths down the mountain are rather narrow.
5. Why does she keep such an unusually neat desk?
6. All of us were thoroughly nervous before the test.
7. An especially sweet neighbor brought fruit.
8. How much taller is he than I?
9. The choir members were overly tired.
10. That's far too valuable to take on the trip.

REVIEW EXERCISE

A., page 115

	VERB	WORDS CONNECTED
a.v.	1. Can picture	
a.v.	2. ruled	
a.v.	3. had	
a.v.	4. have been preserved	
l.v.	5. might have felt	skin, scaly
l.v.	6. were	dinosaurs, huge
l.v.	7. might have been	dinosaurs, warm-blooded
l.v.	8. were	plant-eaters, size
a.v.	9. do know	
l.v.	10. will remain	appearance, mystery

B., page 115
(Answers will vary. Possible responses are given.)
1. The team had gone to the stadium early.

2. It was quite an enjoyable trip.
3. The deer ran quickly across the meadow.
4. During the storm the girls went inside.
5. Did Carlos buy the tickets today?

C., page 116
(Answers will vary. Possible responses are given. You may want to suggest that students use the charts on pages 109 and 113.)
1. Stretch your arms above your head. (Stretch/action verb)
2. Your hands should be open, with the palms forward. (should be/linking verb)
3. Your legs should remain relaxed, but steady. (should remain/linking verb)
4. Gently bend at the waist, first to the left, then to the right. (bend/action verb)
5. Your muscles may feel tighter after this exercise! (may feel/linking verb)

PREPOSITIONS
EXERCISE 10, page 118
(Answers will vary. Possible responses are given.)
1. behind
2. near
3. through
4. next to
5. under
6. in
7. beside
8. for
9. at
10. over

EXERCISE 11, page 118
1. prep.
2. prep.
3. adv.
4. prep.
5. adv.

CONJUNCTIONS AND INTERJECTIONS
EXERCISE 12, page 120
1. Both, and
2. but
3. Not only, but also
4. yet
5. Neither, nor, for

EXERCISE 13, page 120
(Answers will vary. Possible responses are given.)
1. Oh! I hope this is not the director's last film.
2. Oops! I forgot the leading lady could be the murderer.
3. Ouch! I bet that fall hurt!
4. Ugh, I'd hate to land in that puddle.
5. Well, the actors were well-suited to their roles.

CHAPTER REVIEW
A., page 121
1. v.
2. intj.
3. prep.
4. adv.
5. conj.
6. intj.
7. adv.
8. v.
9. conj.
10. prep.

B., page 121
ACTION VERB	LINKING VERB
1. carried	
2. gave	
3. helped	
4. is building	
5. are moving	
6.	tastes
7.	has become
8. showed	
9.	are
10.	is, is

C., page 122
1. prep., adv.
2. adv., adv.
3. prep., prep.
4. prep., adv.
5. adv., adv.

D., page 122
(Answers will vary. Possible responses are given.)
1. The science test was very <u>hard</u>.—adjective
   Pearly whacked the ball quite <u>hard</u>.—adverb
2. Haven't I met you <u>before</u>?—adverb
   Leon did his exercise <u>before</u> breakfast.—preposition
3. After the storm my puppy was <u>so</u> wet.—adverb
   Tanya pushed the canoe across the river <u>so</u> we could miss the rapids.—conjunction
4. We rehearsed daily, <u>yet</u> we were not prepared.—conjunction.
   The runners have not started <u>yet</u>.—adverb
5. <u>Well</u>, can you believe it?—interjection
   Are you <u>well</u> today?—adjective

CHAPTER 13: COMPLEMENTS
DIRECT OBJECTS
EXERCISE 1, page 124
1. dog
2. wallet, jacket
3. brother
4. rules
5. movie
6. questions
7. directions
8. Spanish, French
9. message
10. air

EXERCISE 2, page 124
(Answers will vary. Possible responses are given.)
1. baseball
2. helicopter
3. Ryan
4. football
5. curve ball
6. race
7. party
8. awards
9. players
10. soccer

INDIRECT OBJECTS
EXERCISE 3, page 125

	I.O.	D.O.
1.	dog	trick
2.	them	map
3.	me	ride
4.	class	poem
5.	us	address
6.	me	postcard
7.	Kim, Filbert	story
8.	neighbors	vegetables
9.	hikers	warning
10.	sister, brother	jacket

19

EXERCISE 4, page 126

1. Minnie told <u>us</u> the whole story.
2. Last month, she wrote the <u>city council</u> a letter.
3. She gave <u>them</u> several ideas about summer <u>programs</u> for kids.
4. They offered <u>Minnie</u> and her <u>classmates</u> summer jobs.
5. Together, the class taught the neighborhood <u>children</u> many games.
6. They also offered the <u>children</u> swimming lessons.
7. The city owed <u>Minnie</u> many thanks for her ideas and her organizational skills.
8. The neighborhood parents bought <u>Minnie</u> a trophy.
9. All the children brought <u>Minnie</u> and the swimming <u>coaches</u> cards and banners.
10. Minnie had given the <u>city</u> a summer of fun.

PREDICATE NOMINATIVES

EXERCISE 5, page 128

	L.V.	P.N.
1.	was	actor
2.	is	Robert De Niro
3.	has become	director
4.	was	he
5.	is	actress, singer, dancer
6.	might be	*West Side Story*
7.	were	Natalie Wood, George Chakiris, Richard Beymer
8.	is	version
9.	were	"Tonight," "Maria"
10.	was	Leonard Bernstein

EXERCISE 6, page 128

(Answers will vary. Possible responses are given.)

1. An encyclopedia is a reference book.
2. My best friends are Lisette and Jobelle.
3. Some industrial gases are argon, nitrogen, helium, and neon.
4. This rock is granite.
5. The winners of the award for best short story will be Mina and I.

PREDICATE ADJECTIVES

EXERCISE 7, page 129

	L.V.	P.A.
1.	smells	good
2.	is	cloudy, dark
3.	is	funny
4.	became	limp, wilted
5.	remained	brave

EXERCISE 8, page 129

(Answers will vary. Possible responses are given.)

1. The oranges weren't <u>ripe</u>.
2. That dog is always <u>wet</u>.
3. My doctor usually seems <u>friendly</u>.
4. Julio felt <u>sick</u>.
5. Soccer can be <u>exciting</u>.

REVIEW EXERCISE

A., page 130

1. d.o.
2. pred. adj.
3. pred. nom.
4. pred. adj.
5. d.o.

B., page 130

(Answers will vary. Possible responses are given.)

1. Most volcanoes are cone-shaped _____. (mountains; predicate nominative)
2. Powerful forces inside earth cause _____. (volcanoes; direct object)
3. Melted rock deep in the earth is called _____. (magma; direct object)
4. When rock melts, it produces _____. (gas; direct object)
5. The gas-filled magma is _____ than the solid rock around it. (lighter; predicate adjective)

CHAPTER REVIEW

A., page 131

1.	teacher	p.n.
2.	feelings	d.o.
3.	program	d.o.
4.	simple, wise	p.a.
5.	people	d.o.
6.	knowledgeable	p.a.
7.	them	i.o.
	chance	d.o.
8.	"Group Conversation"	p.n.
9.	Martin Luther King, Jr.; Eleanor Roosevelt; George Washington Carver	p.n.
10.	program	d.o.

B., page 132

(Answers will vary. Possible responses are given.)

1. My favorite singer is <u>Whitney Houston</u>.
2. The river is <u>wide</u> and <u>deep</u>.
3. Ms. Robinson made <u>Jim</u> and <u>Elise</u> some <u>sandwiches</u>.
4. Two important historical figures are <u>Jane Addams</u> and <u>Florence Nightingale</u>.
5. The weather today is <u>sunny</u>.

C., page 132

(Answers will vary. Possible responses are given.)

1. Profile: Abdul plays <u>basketball</u> with the Phoenix Suns. He is a <u>guard</u>.
   Complements used: basketball—d.o.; guard—p.n.
2. Profile: Etta May is a <u>doctor</u>. She has a private <u>practice</u> in Detroit.
   Complements used: doctor—p.n.; practice—d.o.
3. Profile: Pauline flies <u>planes</u>. She is a <u>pilot</u> with Overseas Airlines.
   Complements used: planes—d.o.; pilot—p.n.
4. Profile: Otis is a published <u>author</u>. His latest book is <u>Adventures in Spain</u>.
   Complements used: author—p.n.; *Adventures in Spain*—p.n.

CHAPTER 14: THE PHRASE

PREPOSITIONAL PHRASES

EXERCISE 1, page 133

	PREP.	PREP. PHRASE
1.	about	about comfort
2.	in	in a shoe's style and color
3.	Over	Over the years
4.	with	with open toes

5. of	of Rome	
6. during	during the Middle Ages	
7. in	in wide, floppy shoes	
8. on	on their armor	
9. from	from rough weather	
10. In; with	In recent years; with fancy designs and bright colors	

EXERCISE 2, page 134

	OBJECT	PREP. PHRASE
1.	Rosa	except Rosa
2.	them	to them
3.	state	of a state
4.	world	in the world
5.	Southeast Asia	from Southeast Asia

EXERCISE 3, page 134

(Answers will vary. Possible responses are given.)

1. The clown had a dove <u>under his hat</u>.
2. <u>At that moment</u> the sky grew dark, and I heard a sound like that of a freight train.
3. I want a dog <u>with brown eyes</u>.
4. Central Park, as the name implies, is in the center <u>of the city</u>.
5. Yolanda and Ted went <u>to the mall</u>.

ADJECTIVE PHRASES
EXERCISE 4, page 135

	ADJ. PHRASE	WORD MODIFIED
1.	in the photograph	man
2.	to society	contributions
3.	of migrant labor camps; of his youth	series; scene
4.	for migrant farm workers	conditions
5.	to them	dedication
6.	against the California growers	strike
7.	of the strike leaders	one
8.	of the United Farm Workers	organizer
9.	about Chavez's early struggles	Stories
10.	about him	articles

EXERCISE 5, page 136

	ADJ. PHRASE	WORD MODIFIED
1.	of the seaside town	view
2.	of whitewashed stone; to the pier	Houses; road
3.	with long tails	kites
4.	from one; of the islands	boat; one
5.	to the island	visit

EXERCISE 6, page 136

(Answers will vary. Possible responses are given.)

1. On the beach I saw a crab <u>with long legs</u>.
2. I like the design <u>on the green carpet</u>.
3. Peru is on the western coast <u>of South America</u>.
4. Dorinda writes newspaper articles <u>about sports and medicine</u>.
5. The trophies were on the table <u>between the four students</u>.

ADVERB PHRASES
EXERCISE 7, page 137

	ADV. PHRASE	WORD MODIFIED
1.	in nature	common
2.	for long periods	can travel
3.	Across northern Canada	migrate
4.	in herds	live
5.	into open areas; for food	move; look
6.	for the woods	head
7.	on small plants	feed
8.	for great distances	can fly
9.	In a single year	travel
10.	after the long trip	soon
11.	near the Arctic Circle	nest
12.	for Antarctica; in the autumn	leave leave
13.	With small radios	have mapped
14.	During its lifetime	may travel
15.	over long distances	carry
16.	to the North	return
17.	in stages	make
18.	at small ponds; for food and water	stop stop
19.	In the air	lead
20.	in protected positions	fly

EXERCISE 8, page 138

(Answers will vary. Possible responses are given.)

1. <u>In the rain forest</u> the scientists <u>collected</u> rare plants.
2. Chandra <u>bought</u> a CD player <u>with her savings</u>.
3. The dog <u>hid</u> under the old bed.
4. <u>At four o'clock</u> the great cathedral bell <u>rang</u>.
5. The uniforms <u>were chosen</u> <u>by the team</u>.
6. <u>After the long movie</u>, we <u>went</u> home.

REVIEW EXERCISE 1
A., page 139

	PREP. PHRASE	PREP.	OBJECT
1.	in Mei-Ling's life	in	life
2.	in the Air Force	in	Air Force
3.	near Los Angeles	near	Los Angeles
4.	During the first weeks; through basic training	During; through	weeks; training
5.	After that time; for certain jobs	After; for	time; jobs
6.	to a special school	to	school
7.	in radar	in	radar
8.	of space medicine	of	medicine
9.	Within a few months; of assignments	Within; of	months; assignments
10.	in the Air Force	in	Air Force

B., page 139

	PREP. PHR.	TYPE	WORD MODIFIED
1.	in a spacecraft	adj.	Life
2.	from the air	adv.	removes
3.	of the air	adj.	temperature
4.	for astronauts	adj.	problem
5.	On long space missions	adv.	must exercise

C., page 140

(Answers will vary. Possible response is given.)

1. Place the couch in front of the south window.

ADV. PHRASE	ADJ. PHRASE
1. in front	of the south window

21

VERB PHRASES AND VERBALS
EXERCISE 9, page 141
1. a. v.
   b. v.phr.
2. a. v.
   b. v.phr.
3. a. v.phr.
   b. v.
4. a. v.phr.
   b. v.
5. a. v.
   b. v.phr.

EXERCISE 10, page 142
(Answers will vary. Possible responses are given.)
1. a. was driving
   b. driving
2. a. hidden
   b. has been hiding
3. a. lost
   b. were losing
4. a. will be cooking
   b. cooked
5. a. Worrying
   b. were worrying

PARTICIPLES AND PARTICIPIAL PHRASES
EXERCISE 11, page 143

PARTICIPLE	WORD MODIFIED
1. fallen	tree
2. setting	sun
3. buried	treasure
4. deserted	village
5. winning	ticket

EXERCISE 12, page 144

PART. PHR.	WORD MODIFIED
1. lining the canyons	ruins
2. Dating from the thirteenth century	they
3. known as pueblos	ruins
4. Developing their skills	people
5. working hard	people
6. started in A.D. 920	Pueblo Bonita
7. connecting each level	ladders
8. using dry-land farming	Anasazi
9. lasting for many years	drought
10. Abandoning these homes	Anasazi

INFINITIVES AND INFINITIVE PHRASES
EXERCISE 13, page 145
1. to travel
2. to learn
3. To leave
4. to memorize
5. To prepare
6. to repair
7. To escape
8. to practice
9. To succeed
10. to read

EXERCISE 14, page 146
1. to protect themselves in many ways
2. to match their surroundings
3. to change its color for protection
4. to play tricks on their enemies
5. to escape their enemies
6. To replace their old tails
7. to fly short distances
8. to sail from tree limb to tree limb
9. to defend themselves
10. to whip its enemy

REVIEW EXERCISE 2
A., page 147

VERBAL	TYPE
1. Exhausted	part.
2. to interview	inf.
3. to rest	inf.
4. frozen	part.
5. laughing	part.
6. To succeed	inf.
7. to answer	inf.
8. Broken	part.
9. to find	inf.
10. challenging	part.

B., page 147

PHRASE	TYPE
1. to circle the sun once	inf.
2. to imagine a world like Jupiter	inf.
3. Covered by thick clouds	part.
4. swirling constantly	part.
5. discovered three hundred years ago	part.
6. to vary in color	inf.
7. to photograph the surface of Jupiter	inf.
8. to get a close-up view of the planet	inf.
9. Moving at great speeds	part.
10. To reach the distant planet	inf.

C., page 148
(Answers will vary. Possible responses are given.)

My favorite place is the movie house <u>located in the center of town</u> (part. phr.). I come here every weekend <u>to see movies about foreign countries</u> (inf. phr.). <u>Hearing different languages and music</u> (part. phr.) makes me want <u>to travel</u> (inf. phr.). <u>Redecorating the building</u> (part phr.) was a big project last year. <u>To get to the balcony,</u> (inf. phr.) you had <u>to climb a wide spiral staircase.</u> (inf. phr.)

CHAPTER REVIEW
A., page 149

PREP.	OBJECT	WORD/PHR. MODIFIED
1. from	scraps	made
2. of	fruits	bowl
3. behind	house	hill
4. During	World War I	dug
5. for without	years water	can live can live
6. in	morning	Early
7. between	toad, frog	difference
8. with	sides	polygon
9. Instead of	paste	buy
10. for	tulips	famous

B., page 149

PHRASE	TYPE
1. for hot-air balloon trips	prep. phr.

22

2. on an adventurous trip — prep. phr.
3. Guided by wind currents; — verbal phr.
   by wind currents; — prep. phr.
   over the mountain — prep. phr.
4. To float over the snow-clad Alps; — verbal phr.
   over the snow-clad Alps — prep. phr.
5. to make a hot-air balloon flight — verbal phr.

C., page 150

PHRASE — TYPE

1. To record language; — inf. phr.
   in civilization's development — prep. phr.
2. of true writing; — prep. phr.
   about five thousand years ago — prep. phr.
3. Living in Mesopotamia; — part. phr.
   in Mesopotamia; — prep. phr.
   into wet clay tablets; — prep. phr.
   to make impressions — inf. phr.
4. of writing; — prep. phr.
   known as cuneiform; — part. phr.
   by the Babylonians — prep. phr.
5. to learn the history of the Sumerians; — inf. phr.
   of the Sumerians — prep. phr.

CHAPTER 15: THE CLAUSE

INDEPENDENT AND SUBORDINATE CLAUSES

EXERCISE 1, page 151
1. sub.
2. indep.
3. sub.
4. sub.
5. indep.
6. indep.
7. sub.
8. indep.
9. indep.
10. indep.

EXERCISE 2, page 152
(Answers will vary. Possible responses are given.)
1. <u>The student</u> who wrote this report <u>received a high mark.</u>
2. <u>Signal to the orchestra</u> when you're ready.
3. <u>The audience cheered</u> as the winners were announced.
4. If you want tickets to the concept, <u>I can buy them.</u>

THE ADJECTIVE CLAUSE
EXERCISE 3, page 153
1. whom founded a ballet company
2. who looked familiar
3. that is having the sale on blank tapes
4. which was taken in 1953
5. whose name you have picked
6. who looked tired
7. that I'm using
8. which belongs to my older sister
9. whom we met
10. that looks different

EXERCISE 4, page 154

ADJ. CL. — REL. PRON.

1. that I've seen — that
2. whose voice you hear — whose
3. which is complicated — which
4. whom you saw in the first act — whom
5. that you heard — that
6. who replaced the singer — who
7. that tells the plot of this opera — that
8. which moves up and down — which
9. who designed the sets — who
10. that you recognized — that

EXERCISE 5, page 154
(Answers will vary. Possible responses are given.)
1. The runner who won the race is being interviewed.
2. Aunt Sylvia is a talented woman whom I admire.
3. Here is the soup, which is my favorite part of the meal.
4. We studied an animal that is extinct.

THE ADVERB CLAUSE
EXERCISE 6, page 156
1. Since I was in the first grade
2. as much as I can
3. while I was reading about Pluto
4. Before astronomers discovered Pluto's moon in 1978
5. Although Pluto is tiny
6. Because Pluto is small
7. because scientists have used the Hubble Space Telescope to observe it.
8. as if some other small planet were nearby
9. Unless scientists develop stronger telescopes
10. When the New Horizons space craft flies near Pluto

CHAPTER REVIEW
A., page 157
1. sub.
2. indep.
3. sub.
4. sub.
5. indep.
6. sub.
7. sub.
8. indep
9. sub.
10. sub.

B., page 157
1. adv.—before they had telephones
2. adj.—that they hit with sticks
3. adj.—who lived far away
4. adj.—that were made from animal skin
5. adv.—Because the drums were different shapes and sizes
6. adv.—Although sound was used by some people
7. adj.—that some Chinese, Egyptian, and Native Americans used
8. adv.—if they were sent at night
9. adv.—After electricity was discovered
10. adj.—who work in large companies

C., page 158
(Answers will vary. Responses should contain at least five adjective and five adverb clauses.)

CHAPTER 16: SENTENCE STRUCTURE

SIMPLE SENTENCES
EXERCISE 1, page 159

	S.	V.
1.	mountains; forests	provide
2.	Andes Mountains	separate
3.	point	is
4.	coastline	stretches
5.	people	speak; belong
6.	Manufacturing; mining	have grown; have become
7.	Plantations; farms; ranches	cover; employ
8.	Coffee; bananas	are
9.	South America	exports; imports
10.	Silver; copper	are
11.	animals; birds	live
12.	capybara	grows; is
13.	snake	lives; swims
14.	turtles	live
15.	tapir	is

EXERCISE 2, page 160
(Answers will vary. Possible responses are given.)
1. My favorite <u>book</u> <u>is</u> *The Red Pony*.
2. Yesterday <u>Marlene</u> and <u>I</u> <u>ate</u> lunch together and then <u>went</u> bowling.
3. Should <u>Albert</u> <u>write</u> or <u>type</u> his report?
4. <u>Dr. Glynn</u> <u>gave</u> an interesting talk on the U.S. space program.
5. <u>Frances</u> and <u>Julio</u> <u>are bringing</u> baseballs for our games.

COMPOUND SENTENCES
EXERCISE 3, page 161

	S.	V.	CONNECTOR
1.	people they	could record had invented	for
2.	people people	made could stay	yet
3.	Ice sheets people	lowered traveled	; as a result
4.	trend seas	melted began	so
5.	Hunters group	built would live	for
6.	campsite group others	would be divided used were used	; and
7.	campsites these	had give	and
8.	tools others	were made were made	;
9.	Farming people	was developed hunted, collected	so
10.	farmers they	grew hunted	yet
11.	hunters group	lived consisted	and
12.	families all	shared hunted	but
13.	group it	moved met	yet

14. Hunters   developed   ; therefore,
    animals   could be captured, killed
15. Scientists   have pieced   but
    questions   are

EXERCISE 4, page 162
(Answers will vary. Possible responses are given.)
1. <u>Manuel</u> <u>entered</u> his sketches in an art contest; the <u>judging</u> <u>is</u> tomorrow.
2. Severe <u>thunderstorms</u> <u>are predicted</u> for this afternoon; therefore, our soccer <u>game</u> <u>will be rescheduled</u>.
3. <u>Bly</u> and <u>Mato</u> <u>paddled</u> hard, but at nightfall <u>they</u> <u>were</u> still miles from camp.
4. The <u>gardener</u> <u>watered</u> everything in the yard, for <u>it</u> <u>wasn't</u> likely to rain until next week.
5. Surely <u>we</u> <u>made</u> the right choice, or <u>we</u> <u>could be</u> in trouble.

EXERCISE 5, page 163

	TYPE	S.	V.
1.	comp.	Muslims mosques	pray are
2.	simp.	courtyard, hall	are
3.	comp.	hall it	has has
4.	simp.	call	was delivered, comes
5.	comp.	mosque some	has have
6.	comp.	Syria, countries those	have have
7.	simp.	builders	imitated, used
8.	comp.	mosques none	have have
9.	simp.	Flowers, designs	are permitted, ornament
10.	comp.	mosques Istanbul	combine has

EXERCISE 6, page 164
1. <u>Cardinals</u> and <u>blue jays</u> <u>gathered</u> around our bird feeder.
2. <u>Squirrels</u> <u>scurried</u> up a nearby tree and <u>jumped</u> through the air to the bird feeder.
3. The <u>food</u> and <u>water</u> <u>disappeared</u> quickly and <u>needed</u> daily attention.
4. My <u>brother</u> and <u>I</u> <u>moved</u> the bird feeder to another tree, and the <u>squirrels</u> <u>followed</u> close behind.
5. <u>We</u> <u>decided</u> to move it away from the trees, so <u>we</u> <u>hung</u> the feeder from a clothesline pole and <u>greased</u> the pole.

COMPLEX SENTENCES
EXERCISE 7, page 165

	SUB. CL.	SUB. CONJ.	REL. PRON.
1.	who ate the acorns of the tree		who
2.	which can grow to a height of one hundred feet		which
3.	because it played an important role in the early history of the Connecticut colony	because	
4.	who was king of England		who
5.	that Charles II gave the colony		that

6. who was the governor of the Dominion of New England — who
7. When he arrived in Connecticut in 1687 — When
8. Since the colonists valued their freedom — Since
9. which is now called the Charter Oak — which
10. Although historians are not sure of all the facts — Although

EXERCISE 8 page 166
(Answers will vary. Possible responses are given.)
1. <u>Because the alarm did not go off</u>, I was late for school.
2. <u>When the cherry trees are in bloom</u>, tourists descend on the nation's capital.
3. <u>Though Bessie studied Italian</u>, she could not understand Mario's dialect.
4. Rodrigo, <u>who is president of his class</u>, was born in Ecuador.
5. We went to the football game, <u>which was broadcast on television</u>.

CHAPTER REVIEW
A., page 167

INDEP. CL.	SUB. CL.
1. Jim Thorpe was one of the greatest athletes of all time	who was a Native American
2. she proofread it	Before Isabel gave her story to the editor
3. the quarterback threw the ball down the field for a touchdown	As we watched in the last few minutes of the game
4. Robert Moses was commissioner of New York parks	when the Verrazano-Narrows Bridge was built
5. we headed for the harbor	Because heavy winds whipped up the water in the bay
6. My brother pointed the remote control at the television set	while he switched from channel to channel
7. its overall shape has not changed	Although the grand piano was invented more than one hundred years ago
8. Oases vary in size	which are fertile areas in the desert
9. Charlene wants a job this summer	so that she can start saving money for college
10. Jupiter is the largest planet in the solar system	which is the fifth planet from the sun

B., page 167
1. cx.
2. comp.
3. simp.
4. cx.
5. cx.
6. simp.
7. cx.
8. cx.
9. simp.
10. comp.

C., page 168
(Answers will vary. Possible responses are given.)
1. Do you prefer peaches or plums?
2. Carlisle and Rudy washed and waxed their mother's car.
3. We visited the Wongs, and they showed us around their farm.
4. Serena wants to get a job after school, but her parents want her to study piano instead.
5. The person who has the highest grade-point average will be the class valedictorian.

CHAPTER 17: AGREEMENT

AGREEMENT OF SUBJECT AND VERB
EXERCISE 1, page 169
1. pl.
2. sing.
3. sing.
4. pl.
5. sing.

EXERCISE 2, page 170

S.	V.
1. oysters	create
2. They	join
3. trees	sprout
4. party	has
5. foods	contain
6. brother	asks
7. they	serve
8. I	like
9. you	are
10. hamster	runs
11. Eric	makes
12. game	has
13. volunteer	promises
14. parents	are
15. candles	glow

INTERVENING PREPOSITIONAL PHRASES
EXERCISE 3, page 171

S.	V.	PREP. PHR.
1. Children	want	from all over the neighborhood
2. library	contains	near the White House
3. speech	was	during the lunch period
4. Statue of Liberty	stands	in Paris, like the one in New York City
5. Loretta	eats	along with her two friends
6. books	need	next to the window
7. One	sticks	of the wheels on my in-line skates
8. Sheila	is	but not her brother
9. mountains	belong	in the distance
10. gentleman	looks	with the red bow tie

EXERCISE 4, page 172
1. is buried
2. live
3. lies
4. weigh
5. (correct)
6. (correct)
7. live
8. (correct)
9. grows
10. remain

25

EXERCISE 5, page 172

(Answers will vary. The list should contain comments about toys, employees, and the toy store. The sentences should be about the comments in the list. The subject and verb of each sentence should be identified properly and show correct agreement.)

SINGULAR AND PLURAL INDEFINITE PRONOUNS

EXERCISE 6, page 173

1. has
2. gets
3. works
4. answers
5. catches
6. guards
7. writes
8. gets
9. is
10. is

EXERCISE 7, page 174

1. are
2. have
3. are
4. have
5. are
6. want
7. were
8. have
9. know
10. were
11. are
12. match
13. attend
14. belong
15. Do

ALL, ANY, MOST, NONE, AND SOME

EXERCISE 8, page 175

1. offer
2. work
3. has
4. raise
5. is
6. grow
7. seems
8. Do
9. need
10. help

EXERCISE 9, page 176

1. sound
2. gets
3. is
4. (correct)
5. stay
6. (correct)
7. is
8. want
9. like
10. are

EXERCISE 10, page 176

1. was
2. are
3. play
4. appears
5. write

REVIEW EXERCISE

A., page 177

1. has
2. know
3. produces
4. is
5. vacation
6. extend
7. enjoy
8. worries
9. know
10. is

B., page 177

1. have
2. are
3. is
4. aim
5. wants
6. visits
7. were
8. was
9. exist
10. (correct)

C., page 178

(Answers will vary. This exercise will be satisfactorily completed if the student writes five factual sentences about the past four presidents of the United States. The subjects and verbs in these sentences should agree.)

COMPOUND SUBJECTS

EXERCISE 11, page 179

1. want
2. are
3. are
4. take
5. is
6. Do
7. are
8. are
9. watch
10. live

EXERCISE 12, page 180

1. were
2. are
3. was
4. is
5. allows
6. Has
7. helps
8. has
9. sell
10. mentions

COLLECTIVE NOUNS AND INVERTED SENTENCES

EXERCISE 13, page 182

1. lives
2. stays
3. has appeared
4. are voting
5. like
6. performs
7. debate
8. does
9. lives
10. was

EXERCISE 14, page 182

S.	V.
1. day	is
2. solstice	Is
3. solstices	are
4. day	Was
5. celebrations	are
6. key	lies
7. brothers	come
8. tomatoes	Are
9. reasons	are
10. excuse	is

AMOUNTS, TITLES, AND DON'T AND DOESN'T

EXERCISE 15, page 183

1. is
2. seems
3. is
4. Is
5. is
6. equals
7. has
8. seems
9. does
10. receives

EXERCISE 16, page 184

(This exercise will be satisfactorily completed if the student writes five sentences about different farm or domestic animals. Each sentence should have a different subject, and each should contain the word *don't* or the word *doesn't* used in correct agreement with the subject. The sentences should tell what the animals do or don't eat or how they do or don't behave.)

PRONOUN-ANTECEDENT AGREEMENT

EXERCISE 17, page 186

ANTE.	PRON.
1. Kitty; Bruno	their
2. Vern; Mr. Park	his
3. One	its
4. Vern; Kitty	their
5. Dawn; Sabrena	her
6. Each	his *or* her
7. Mrs. Park; mother	their

8. Anyone — he *or* she
9. script — its
10. actors — their

CHAPTER REVIEW
A., page 187
1. are
2. are made
3. has
4. digs
5. were built
6. is
7. (*correct*)
8. (*correct*)
9. are working
10. is being used

B., page 187
1. his *or* her
2. their
3. his
4. its
5. he *or* she; his *or* her
6. his
7. their
8. (*correct*)
9. his *or* her
10. (*correct*)

C., page 188
(This exercise will be satisfactorily completed if the student writes at least two sentences about animals that protect themselves with color matching and shape matching. Subjects and verbs must agree.)

CHAPTER 18: USING VERBS CORRECTLY

PRINCIPAL PARTS
EXERCISE 1, page 190
1. pres.
2. past
3. past
4. past
5. pres.
6. fut.
7. fut.
8. past
9. pres.
10. fut.

EXERCISE 2, page 190
1. base
2. pres. part.
3. past
4. pres. part
5. base
6. past part.
7. past
8. past part.
9. past
10. base

REGULAR VERBS
EXERCISE 3, page 191

PRES. PART.	PAST	PAST PART.
1. (is) looking	looked	(have) looked
2. (is) selecting	selected	(have) selected
3. (is) shopping	shopped	(have) shopped
4. (is) using	used	(have) used
5. (is) starting	started	(have) started

EXERCISE 4, page 192
(Answers will vary. Possible responses are given.)
1. I am hoping that the team will win.
2. Bob has enjoyed the trip.
3. Yesterday I dropped your library book into the book-return box.
4. He has raised his hand twice to answer the question.
5. We are slipping on the icy sidewalks.
6. Jim and Kareem have already talked to Sally.
7. He asked an interesting question.
8. He is answering your letter now.
9. This dog followed me home.
10. I am still laughing at your joke.

IRREGULAR VERBS
EXERCISE 5, page 195
1. written
2. won
3. put
4. made
5. knew
6. chose
7. came
8. grew
9. got
10. led
11. began
12. went
13. wrote
14. given
15. sent
16. saw
17. said
18. drawn
19. built
20. taken

EXERCISE 6, page 196
(Answers will vary. Possible responses are given.)
1. How many records <u>have</u> you <u>broken</u>?
2. <u>Have</u> you ever <u>felt</u> nervous before a race?
3. <u>Can</u> you <u>remember</u> when you first <u>knew</u> that you <u>would be</u> a great athlete?
4. In how many swim meets <u>have</u> you <u>swum</u>?
5. How <u>did</u> you <u>feel</u> when you <u>lost</u> that important race last year?
6. How many races <u>have</u> you <u>won</u>?
7. <u>Have</u> you ever <u>hurt</u> your legs during a competition?
8. When you <u>rode</u> a horse for the first time, <u>were</u> you <u>scared</u>?
9. <u>Were</u> people <u>surprised</u> when as a high school student you <u>threw</u> the javelin so well?
10. What advice <u>has</u> your coach <u>given</u> you about training?

TENSE
EXERCISE 7, page 198
(Answers will vary. Possible responses are given.)

 [1] Odessa, Benny, and I were on a hike in the woods, and we got lost. [2] We started up a steep hill. [3] "Oh, no!" I shouted. [4] From the top of the hill, I saw storm clouds. [5] A bad storm was rushing toward us. [6] Looking for cover, we ran down the hill. [7] Then Benny found a small cave in the side of the hill. [8] We climbed in under the big rocks just as the rain started falling. [9] Rain fell for about an hour. [10] During that time, we cheered each other up with jokes and waited for the storm to pass.

SIT AND SET AND RISE AND RAISE
EXERCISE 8, page 199
1. set
2. sit
3. sitting
4. Set
5. sat

EXERCISE 9, page 200
1. raise
2. rise
3. raised
4. rose
5. rising

LIE AND LAY
EXERCISE 10, page 201
1. laid
2. lie
3. lying
4. lay
5. Lay

EXERCISE 11, page 202
1. lay
2. lain
3. laid
4. lying
5. laid
6. lies
7. laid
8. lain
9. Lay
10. laying

EXERCISE 12, page 202
1. lie
2. laid
3. (correct)
4. laid
5. laid

CHAPTER REVIEW
A., page 203
1. sitting
2. rose
3. set
4. laid; set
5. sitting
6. rose
7. raised
8. lying
9. sat
10. rose

B., page 203
1. went
2. began
3. sold
4. rose
5. led
6. has written
7. (correct)
8. tells *or* told
9. gives *or* (correct)
10. have become

C., page 204
(Answers will vary. Possible responses are given.)
Dear Joan,
 You won't believe all the wonderful food I have eaten since I arrived.
 Did you know that Paris is divided by the Seine River?
 I visited the Eiffel Tower in Paris yesterday. It was beautiful. I have taken the streetcar to the Pompidou Center and the Cathedral of Notre Dame. I also walked through the Luxembourg Gardens and rested on the benches on the grounds there.
 I will try to describe the beauty of the Arc de Triomphe. It's a very impressive monument that has beautiful lighting at night.
                    See you soon,
                    Latrice

CHAPTER 19: USING PRONOUNS CORRECTLY

CASE OF PRONOUNS
EXERCISE 1, page 206
1. poss.
2. nom.
3. obj.
4. nom.
5. poss.
6. poss.
7. poss.
8. nom.
9. obj.
10. poss.

NOMINATIVE CASE PRONOUNS
EXERCISE 2, page 208
1. I
2. we
3. he and I
4. They
5. He

EXERCISE 3, page 208
1. she
2. (correct)
3. he and I
4. they
5. (correct)

OBJECTIVE CASE PRONOUNS
EXERCISE 4, page 209
(Answers will vary. Possible responses are given.)
1. me
2. him
3. her
4. him
5. them

EXERCISE 5, page 210
1. me
2. us
3. them
4. us
5. her

EXERCISE 6, page 210
1. (correct)
2. them
3. me
4. (correct)
5. her

PRONOUNS AS OBJECTS OF PREPOSITIONS
EXERCISE 7, page 211
1. me
2. them
3. me
4. us
5. them
6. them
7. him and me
8. us
9. me
10. him

EXERCISE 8, page 212
1. us
2. them
3. her
4. them
5. her *or* him
6. him
7. her
8. us
9. her
10. him

WHO AND WHOM
EXERCISE 9, page 214
1. Who
2. who
3. whom
4. Whom
5. whom
6. Whom
7. whom
8. whom
9. whom
10. Who

EXERCISE 10, page 214
1. (correct)
2. Who
3. whom
4. (correct)
5. Who

PRONOUN APPOSITIVES AND REFLEXIVE PRONOUNS
EXERCISE 11, page 215
1. We
2. us
3. we
4. we
5. us

EXERCISE 12, page 216
1. himself
2. themselves
3. themselves
4. himself
5. himself

CHAPTER REVIEW
A., page 217
1. he
2. themselves
3. Whom
4. me
5. We

B., page 217
1. himself
2. (*correct*)
3. he
4. him; them
5. themselves
6. her
7. he
8. (*correct*)
9. (*correct*)
10. Who
11. (*correct*)
12. (*correct*)
13. me; We
14. (*correct*)
15. they
16. her
17. (*correct*)
18. himself
19. me
20. he

C., page 218
(Interview questions should show correct use of pronouns. Commend responses that show evidence of thorough research and creativity.)

CHAPTER 20: USING MODIFIERS CORRECTLY

COMPARISON OF ADJECTIVES AND ADVERBS
EXERCISE 1, page 220
1. sooner/less soon; soonest/least soon
2. more/less independent; most/least independent
3. wiser/less wise; wisest/least wise
4. more/less lightly; most/least lightly
5. more/less beautiful; most/least beautiful
6. hungrier/less hungry; hungriest/least hungry
7. more/less cautiously; most/least cautiously
8. more/less hopeful; most/least hopeful
9. nicer; nicest
10. more/less shyly; most/least shyly

IRREGULAR COMPARISON
EXERCISE 2, page 221
1. farther
2. more
3. better
4. better
5. most
6. worse
7. farthest
8. most
9. worst
10. better

EXERCISE 3, page 222
1. good
2. many
3. most
4. well
5. best

EXERCISE 4, page 222
(Answers will vary. Sample answers are given.)
1. The plot of *The Last Days on Moffat Island* was the <u>most</u> <u>unbelievable</u> of any movie I've ever seen.
2. The major events couldn't happen <u>more</u> <u>slowly</u> if the movie were a painting.
3. The characters are the <u>dullest</u> and <u>most</u> <u>unlikeable</u> creatures to hit the big screen in some time.
4. The dialogue is <u>more</u> <u>mechanical</u> than a robot's.
5. The ending was <u>more</u> <u>unrealistic</u> than any ending I've ever seen.

SPECIAL PROBLEMS IN USING MODIFIERS
EXERCISE 5, page 223
1. well
2. quickly
3. good
4. quiet
5. good
6. fresh
7. strong
8. good
9. well
10. carefully

EXERCISE 6, page 224
1. quickly
2. happy
3. good
4. careful
5. good
6. quickly
7. slowly
8. well
9. closely
10. sad

DOUBLE COMPARISONS
EXERCISE 7, page 225
(Answers will vary. Possible responses are given.)
1. Jon had never been out of the country.
2. Penny will never forget her best friend.
3. Traffic is heaviest around five o'clock in the afternoon.
4. Ted isn't going to the meeting either.
5. The baby was quieter than a mouse.
6. Are you working longer than you used to?
7. I am not doing anything tonight.
8. Hasn't James ever seen the ocean?
9. Dominique could never be mean to anyone.
10. Of all the members of the basketball team, Antonio is the shortest.

EXERCISE 8, page 226
(Answers may vary. Possible responses are given.)
1. The Mbuti use nothing but leaves and branches to build a village.
2. A woman starts building a hut by making a dome from the younger trees in a clearing.
3. Leaves cover this dome, keeping out the worst rain and winds.
4. The Mbuti never live more than two months in one place.
5. They move on to make a new village where food sources are closer.

PLACEMENT OF MODIFIERS
EXERCISE 9, page 228
(Some answers will vary. Possible responses are given.)
1. The girl from next door is jogging around the park.
2. The boy in blue polka-dot shorts was riding on a bicycle.
3. She gave the gift with the pink wrapping paper to the boy.

4. I heard a report on the radio that a bad storm is coming.
5. The train from San Diego arrived after we had lunch.

EXERCISE 10, page 228
1. Elaine put the shirt with green stripes on the baby.
2. The monkey in the tree was chattering at the children.
3. The girl with pigtails is making a dress.
4. We learned from Aunt Melanie that a big blizzard was coming.
5. The boy with the red boots was walking the dog.

PLACEMENT OF PARTICIPIAL PHRASES
EXERCISE 11, page 230
1. Deirdre, whose record is outstanding, has earned a scholarship.
2. Listening to the words, I suddenly got tears in my eyes.
3. The dress that you made does not fit me.
4. I heard some of my favorite songs played by the band.
5. Wearing a raincoat and boots, the man hurried through the store.
6. Camping at the river, Ms. Cuomo saw two owls.
7. Sitting under that shady tree, I've written some of my best poems.
8. Driving along the freeway, we saw a herd of deer.
9. The Battle of Saratoga, which was fought in 1777, saved the American Revolution.
10. At the library, I found a book that was written by Amy Tan.

CHAPTER REVIEW
A., page 231
1. At the party, he told us that he had saved his allowance for a year to buy the bike.
2. Some scientists think asteroids hurtling through space will someday hit the earth.
3. Driving to the mall, we discovered a shortcut.
4. An orange that had been peeled lay on the table.
5. I got a dog that is only six weeks old from the animal shelter.

B., page 231

ERROR	CORRECTION
1. most beautifulest	most beautiful
2. couldn't find no	could find no
3. more friendlier	friendlier
4. well	good
5. good	well
6. can't scarcely	can scarcely
7. larger	largest
8. smallest	smaller
9. Much	Many
10. tiredly	tired

C., page 232
(Answers will vary. Responses should use modifiers correctly.)

CHAPTER 21:
A GLOSSARY OF USAGE

ACCEPT / AS (LIKE)
EXERCISE 1, page 234
1. accepted
2. all right
3. all ready
4. aren't
5. excepted
6. already
7. except
8. a lot
9. accept
10. a lot

BETWEEN / HAD OUGHT
EXERCISE 2, page 236
1. Mark would have come to the show, but he caught the flu and doesn't feel well.
2. As I was getting into my costume, the zipper broke.
3. David ought not to lift that piece of stage scenery by himself.
4. Will you bring the magician's rabbit over here to us?
5. Mrs. Adriana divided the pizza among the six of us.
6. Sam felt good because he had fewer tests on Tuesday than Paula did.
7. I wish I could have brought the dog on our trip.
8. I have fewer sponsors than you for the Walk for Hunger.
9. You ought to clean your room before Mom gets home.
10. He burst out laughing when I told him the joke I had just heard.

HISSELF / TRY AND
EXERCISE 3, page 238
1. Will you teach me how to cook these kinds of authentic Mexican dishes, Mrs. Rodríguez?
2. They must have looked at pictures of themselves in the photo album no fewer than ten times.
3. Saburo tried to teach himself some magic tricks quite quickly.
4. Should we try to finish our report by this Wednesday?
5. Sabrina might have decided to study piano as her mother did.
6. That wolf taught its cubs to hunt for themselves.
7. It's too bad; your cousin might have won.
8. These sorts of hand-woven rugs are imported quite often from Afghanistan.

WELL / YOUR, YOU'RE
EXERCISE 4, page 240
1. who
2. you're
3. a word that
4. your
5. who
6. whose
7. that
8. unless
9. well
10. Who's

EXERCISE 5, page 240
(Answers will vary. Sentences should show correct use of glossary entries.)

CHAPTER REVIEW
A., page 241
1. that
2. accepted
3. already
4. shouldn't

5. who
6. bring
7. to
8. have
9. a lot
10. whose

B., page 241

1. Melissa is a shy person who doesn't like a lot of attention.
2. During the extremely cold weather, our water pipes froze, and then they burst.
3. Will Wanda be at the sports banquet to accept her trophy?
4. (correct)
5. They sold fewer tickets to the play than they had hoped.
6. Those types of watches are no longer being made.
7. Salvador tried to wipe himself off after falling in the mud.
8. (correct)
9. I can't believe that you're moving so far away.
10. Mrs. Olivero should have told us that we were having an English quiz today.

C., page 242

(Answers will vary. A possible response is given.)

You <u>should have</u> seen the crew run around <u>as if</u> they were crazed chickens when one of the freshwater pipes <u>burst</u>. Even though it was a <u>really</u> serious problem, I couldn't help laughing at their actions. I guess it surprised me to see such smart people falling over <u>themselves</u> trying to fix the problem.

CHAPTER 22: CAPITAL LETTERS

THE PRONOUN I AND PROPER NOUNS
EXERCISE 1, page 244

1. a.
2. a.
3. b.
4. a.
5. b.

EXERCISE 2, page 244

1. Miami, Florida; morning
2. Faucett Airlines; Puerto Rico
3. I; United States
4. Lima; Peru
5. taxi; Gold Museum

PLACES AND PEOPLE
EXERCISE 3, page 246

1. Tunisia; Africa
2. Boston; Atlantic Ocean; Massachusetts
3. Rosario Ferré; Puerto Rico
4. Carl Sagan
5. Times Square; Fifth Avenue; Forty-second Street
6. United States; South
7. Key West; Gulf of Mexico
8. Colorado River; Grand Canyon National Park
9. west; Washington, D.C.; Blue Ridge Mountains
10. Saturn; Jupiter

GROUPS, ORGANIZATIONS, AND RELIGIONS
EXERCISE 4, page 248

1. Woodman Middle School
2. American Automobile Association; Christmas
3. Chamber of Commerce
4. Congregational Church
5. United States Senate

EXERCISE 5, page 248

1. a.
2. b.
3. a.
4. b.

OBJECTS, EVENTS, STRUCTURES, AND AWARDS
EXERCISE 6, page 250

1. Purple Heart
2. Fourth of July
3. Washington Monument
4. Swiss
5. winter; December
6. Rockport Winter Carnival
7. White House; Lincoln Memorial
8. fall; October
9. *Orient Express*
10. Pulitzer Prize

TITLES
EXERCISE 7, page 252

1. Donna
2. *The Helen Keller Story*; *The Beacon*
3. *The Cattle Driver*; "Ghost Riders in the Sky"
4. Grandfather; "Bridges in the Garden"

FIRST WORDS, PROPER ADJECTIVES, SCHOOL SUBJECTS
EXERCISE 8, page 254

1. English
2. Chinese
3. According
4. The; Reveals; From; An
5. It's

CHAPTER REVIEW
A., page 255

1. doctor; *Contact*
2. I; Biology 1; Mrs.
3. Bancroft Science Fair; Holder Auditorium
4. sister; Hawaiian
5. to; *Titanic*
6. Aunt; college; Midwest
7. Venus; Roman
8. Institute; Forty-seventh Street
9. Red, White, and Blue Company; Labor Day
10. Nikki Giovanni; Tennessee

B., page 256

1. Last; Granville T. Woods Middle School; International Day
2. One; Imani Dobbey; Nigerian
3. Another; Appalachian Mountains

4. My; Ruben; Taj Mahal; Mr. Totsi
5. A; *Daily Word*; "Students Celebrate the World"

C., page 256
(Answers will vary. Students should capitalize correctly.)

CHAPTER 23: PUNCTUATION

END MARKS AND ABBREVIATIONS
EXERCISE 1, page 258

1. !
2. ?
3. .
4. . *or* !
5. ?
6. ?
7. !
8. .
9. ?
10. !

EXERCISE 2, page 258

1. Ms. E. A. Rodríguez
2. Parker Toy Co., Inc.
3. at 4:30 P.M.
4. 5 ft. 10 in. tall
5. *(correct)*
6. weighing 1 lb. 4 oz.
7. at 13185 Mill Stone Dr.
8. *(correct)*
9. *(correct)*
10. Sam Dole, Sr.

COMMAS IN A SERIES
EXERCISE 3, page 260

1. Yori, Bob, and I enjoyed watching the rodeo last Saturday.
2. The actors wore large, colorful masks made of wood.
3. *(correct)*
4. *(correct)*
5. Several teachers volunteered to cook, to serve, and to clean up after the dinner.
6. The bus drove through Arkansas, through Oklahoma, and across Texas.
7. *(correct)*
8. Someone extinguished the campfire, covered it with sand, and drenched it with water.
9. My father used to carry an old, black lunch pail to school.
10. The Japanese gymnast was young, strong, and graceful.
11. *(correct)*
12. Hard work, dedication, and funding have made our project a success.
13. The costumes they wore were long, flowing dresses.
14. The clerk needs to know who you are, where you live, and when you moved here.
15. We need new erasers and more chalk.
16. Have you been to her cool, peaceful garden?
17. *(correct)*
18. *(correct)*
19. In this river you can fish for bass, trout, or sunfish.
20. Where is a store that sells televisions, stereos, and VCRs?

COMMAS WITH COMPOUND SENTENCES
EXERCISE 4, page 261

1. The contest will not take place until June, but we already have four entries.
2. *(correct)*
3. They brought no meat or fish, nor did they miss either one.
4. *(correct)*
5. Our cabin was simple, but it had three rooms.
6. People knew about the tomato, yet they were afraid to eat it.
7. Early Arab people used these numbers, and they taught the numbers to other people.
8. *(correct)*
9. Janell drew the pictures, but another artist wrote the words.
10. We rested for an hour, for we had hiked to the top.

EXERCISE 5, page 262
(Answers will vary. Possible responses are given.)

1. I had plenty to eat, yet I still wanted fruit salad for dessert.
2. My brother practices his violin everyday, so he is a wonderful musician.
3. I made dinner for my mother, and my sister brought her flowers.
4. Janice plays soccer after school, yet she still does her homework.
5. You could walk in the park, or you could walk on the beach.
6. Close the windows tightly, for this evening is supposed to bring wind and showers.
7. My class will pick up trash from the schoolyard, and we will return bottles for recycling.
8. Kieshia could enter her painting in the art show, or she could enter her photographs.
9. The summer is going to be hot, so I should go to the town pool often.
10. The restaurant was crowded Friday night, but the service was still excellent.

COMMAS WITH SENTENCE INTERRUPTERS
EXERCISE 6, page 263

1. n.e.; The Empire State Building, which is featured in that movie, is in New York City.
2. e.; The book that I liked best is by Sandra Cisneros.
3. n.e.; The Monadnock Building, in Chicago, is a beautiful example of nineteenth-century public architecture.
4. n.e.; Massachusetts, a small state in the Northeast, had the first public schools in the American colonies.
5. e.; The plant that is in my room doesn't need much water.
6. n.e.; Mark Juneau, who works on North Street, is a talented hairdresser.
7. n.e.; The White Mountains, which are located in New Hampshire, are beautiful.
8. e.; The bird that you saw by the pond was a snowy egret.
9. e.; The bus driver who drives Bus 48 found my folder.

10. n.e.; Mount Everest, which is located on the border of Tibet and Nepal, is the highest peak in the world.
11. e.; The highway that I talked about is closed.
12. n.e.; My car, which is ten years old, still runs well.
13. n.e.; Edgar Allan Poe, who wrote many horror stories, died at an early age.
14. e.; Is it the woman on my right who is governor?
15. e.; The dress that you sent fits me.
16. n.e.; This matter, which is very private, should not be discussed.
17. e.; The athlete who won the race is Gwen Torrence.
18. n.e.; Emma Willard, who founded the first women's school in the United States, is an interesting subject for research.
19. n.e.; The team's mascot, which is a bear, attends almost every game.
20. e.; Those who lost their tickets must wait outside.

OTHER USES OF THE COMMA
EXERCISE 7, page 265

1. I asked Mr. Hatzidais, my next-door neighbor, about his hobby.
2. Did you know that Sophia, my aunt, used to have a beautiful tree in her yard?
3. The tree, an American elm, died of some disease.
4. Mr. Finkle, a biologist, told me about the disease.
5. Did you know that Dutch elm disease, a fungus, can spread from tree to tree?

EXERCISE 8, page 266

1. , Louise,
2. , however,
3. , I believe,
4. To tell the truth,
5. However,
6. Frank,
7. In fact,
8. Nevertheless,
9. , in my opinion,
10. On the other hand,

MORE USES OF THE COMMA
EXERCISE 9, page 268

1. weekend,
2. Well,
3. (correct)
4. stormy,
5. aisle,
6. Street, Bradenton, 34206,
7. 3, 1995,
8. soft,
9. (correct)
10. day,

EXERCISE 10, page 268

1. On May 24, 1883, the Brooklyn Bridge opened.
2. You may write to me at 700 West State Street, Burley, ID 83318.
3. The Panama Canal first opened for shipping on August 15, 1914, after years of hard work by many individuals.
4. We stopped in San Francisco, California, on our way to Hawaii.
5. It wasn't until November 11, 1918, that World War I finally ended.

REVIEW EXERCISE
A., page 269

1. book, Marta,
2. country, cities,
3. Blackwell, admire,
4. intelligent,
5. doctor,
6. Well,
7. Geneva, New York,
8. Emily, sister,
9. varied, challenging,
10. person, Blackwell,

B., page 269

[1] On an ordinary day in 1869, a large stone man was discovered in Cardiff, New York. [2] Several workers had been digging a well, and they discovered the statue. [3] William Newell, the owner of the property, erected a tent; then he began charging admission. [4] People came from all over to see this statue, which was called the Cardiff Giant. [5] Doctors, historians, and neighbors wondered where it had come from. [6] Newell sent the giant on tour to Albany, Syracuse, Boston, and New York. [7] Then the truth came out. [8] Professor Othniel Marsh, a well-known scholar, reported that the statue had been carved out of gypsum, a material that would have dissolved in a few years. [9] If you want to see it, however, you can. [10] It now rests in the Farmer's Museum in Cooperstown, New York.

C., page 270

(Answers will vary. Possible responses are given.)
Cave dwellers, of course, drew these pictures.
Sheridan, a Civil War general, met the Comanches.
By then, of course, we will have colonies on Mars, Saturn, and Pluto.
Hurry, Fred! There's a glider plane ready to take off!
By the end of the day, I felt as if I'd visited my grandfather's time, his grandfather's time, and even before that.

SEMICOLONS
EXERCISE 11, page 272

1. tusks; a
2. carvings; they
3. materials; this
4. away; first
5. shape; thus,
6. ivory; another
7. ivory; this
8. beautiful; however,
9. soapstone; this
10. walrus; they

COLONS
EXERCISE 12, page 273

(Answers will vary. Possible responses are given.)
1. We have shopped at these stores: Jordan's, Mal's, Bashi's Shoes, and the Corner Closet.
2. I go to bed at 9:00 P.M.
3. "Dear Mr. Rogers:" is the greeting line of this business letter.
4. I am going to the park to play, and I'll be home at 4:30 P.M.
5. Jennifer gave invitations to these people: Jan, Inez, Corázon, and Isoke.

6. Today I am going to read Genesis 1:4–10.
7. The baseball game starts at 4:20 P.M.
8. This summer vacation, I am going to do these things: read, swim, and jog.
9. I go jogging every day at 6:00 P.M.
10. The activities that I enjoy are the following ones: drawing, hockey, dancing, and stamp collecting.

CHAPTER REVIEW
A., page 275
1. ostriches,
2. Arizona, Arkansas, California,
3. large,
4. September 12, 1882,
5. Anaheim, California,
6. ostrich, Frantz, 4,
7. 1911,
8. Feathers, clipped, plucked,
9. feathers, decoration,
10. hats, fans, feather dusters,

B., page 275
My family lived in Japan for two years, and I loved every minute of it. *(or!)* My mother works for a computer company, which sent her there. We moved to Japan on March 5, 2007. While we were there, we lived in three different cities: Tokyo, Yokoyhama, and Asaka. Which city do you think was my favorite? Tokyo was it. *(or !)* Tokyo has parks and gardens that are outstanding. There were numerous restaurants to try, many sports exhibitions to see, and museums to visit. Also, Tokyo, you know, has many museums. These include the following choices: a clock museum, a haiku museum, a toy museum, and a kite museum. The toy museum was certainly my favorite, *(or ;)* Mom, however, liked the haiku museum best.

C., page 276

710 Lakeport Drive
Stony Point, NY 10980
August 22, 2008

Dr. Emil Valdez
3486 Wichita Place
Haverstraw, NY 10927

Dear Dr. Valdez:

My school, Jefferson Junior High, has a science fair every year. This year it will be held on October 10, 2008, at the Warren Auditorium. Fair entries include the following four categories: the heavens, our planet, water, and machines. What a wonderful crowd we had last year! This year, however, we'd like to make the fair even better. This desire to improve our fair is why I am writing to you, Dr. Valdez.

Last month my uncle Lokela heard you speak about diets and young people. He thought you were an excellent speaker, and he found the topic fascinating. Well, my class wants you for its speaker. Would you give the speech at our science fair? We would schedule a time between 1:30 and 3:30 P.M. We could pick you up at the airport, drive you to the fair, and take you back to the airport. We would also include your name on our list of sponsors. I hope you will accept our offer. Please let us know before September 8, 2008.

Sincerely,
Irma Lukas

CHAPTER 24: PUNCTUATION
UNDERLINING (ITALICS)
EXERCISE 1, page 278
1. *Barrio Boy*
2. *I Love Lucy*
3. *San Francisco Examiner*
4. *license*
5. *Snap the Whip*
6. *To Kill a Mockingbird*
7. *The Marriage of Figaro*
8. *p; Mississippi*
9. *Raisin in the Sun*
10. *Galileo*

EXERCISE 2, page 278
1. The Boston Globe; North Shore Record
2. Our Town: Romeo and Juliet
3. The Art of Thornton Wilder: Our Town's
4. Ugly Betty
5. Appledore III

QUOTATION MARKS
EXERCISE 3, page 280
1. "Lim Sing is looking forward to the Festival of Lanterns," said her father.
2. Chen replied, "I received calendars from relatives in Hong Kong."
3. "If you look closely at them," he explained, "you can see each day's lunar date written in Chinese."
4. "Will you help me cook the special roasted seeds and dried fruits Mother bought for the New Year's meal?" asked Lim Sing.
5. "Aunt Wang steamed a whole fish!" exclaimed Chen. "Now she is cooking my favorite pork dish."

EXERCISE 4, page 281
1. "Did you know that the city of Santa Barbara sponsors an Old Spanish Days fiesta in August?" asked Mario.
2. "Last night I read the story "The Last Leaf" to my sister," said Nora.
3. Marion Anderson once sang "America" at the Lincoln Memorial.
4. "Who said, 'An apple a day keeps the doctor away'?" asked Meli.
5. "Our sun is just an ordinary star!" exclaimed Floyd. "It's neither the biggest nor the brightest. However, it's the star nearest earth."
6. Rachel Field wrote a poem called "Snow in the City."
7. Mr. Ryder said, "The last chapter of *Anne of Avonlea* is 'A Wedding at the Stone House.'"
8. Read the article called "Saving the Coast" in the school newspaper.
9. Sarah said, "This will be a busy weekend. We are planting beach grass on the dunes to hold the sand in place. The grass will also help the dunes grow higher."
10. "Didn't the teacher say 'Use your calculator'?" asked Bruce.

EXERCISE 5, page 282
[1] "You have had fish every night this week," Mr. Brooks reminded his son. [2] "I thought that you didn't like fish."

[3] "I don't," replied Felix, "but we're having a big social studies test next week."

[4] "What has that got to do with eating fish?" asked his father as he stood at the sink, peeling potatoes.
[5] "Well," answered Felix, "my friend Ben said, 'Fish is brain food.' [6] If you eat enough fish, you'll become smarter.'"
[7] Mr. Brooks turned and faced his son. [8] "Felix, fish is no better for your brain than any other food. [9] You'll be better off worrying less about your diet and spending more time studying."
[10] "I was afraid of that," Felix replied gloomily.

APOSTROPHES
EXERCISE 6, page 284
1. sailor's
2. captain's
3. seaman's
4. day's
5. galleon's
6. moment's
7. mast's *or* masts'
8. ship's
9. hull's
10. crew's

EXERCISE 7, page 284
1. the carpenters' tools
2. the mice's tails
3. Fatima's towel
4. the coach's office
5. the children's toys

OTHER USES OF THE APOSTROPHE
EXERCISE 8, page 286
1. you're
2. shouldn't
3. (correct)
4. musn't; they're
5. we'll
6. (correct)
7. You'll
8. Let's
9. Don't
10. you're

EXERCISE 9, page 286
1. can't
2. there's
3. What's
4. I'm
5. It's

CHAPTER REVIEW
A., page 287
1. "What does the word symbol that begins with an s mean?" asked Leroy.
2. "Did you know that a, b, c, and d are symbols?" asked Jesse. "All letters stand for sounds."
3. "Numbers are symbols, too," added Cora. "When you write 5's and 7's and 9's, you're writing symbols."
4. "Countries also have symbols," said Jesse. "The United States has lots of symbols. Uncle Sam's one of them."
5. "You've probably seen him," added Cora. "He's a tall, skinny cartoon character in a red-white-and-blue suit."
6. "The first cartoons of Uncle Sam didn't appear until the 1830s," added Jesse. "But a book titled The Adventures of Uncle Sam had appeared in '16."
7. "One clever cartoon of him appeared on the cover of The Saturday Evening Post in 1927," said Cora.
8. "He was wearing a pilot's helmet," explained Jesse, "in honor of Charles Lindbergh's flight across the Atlantic in the Spirit of St. Louis."
9. "Didn't Uncle Sam say, 'I Want YOU'?" asked Leroy. "I think that the government used Uncle Sam to get people to join the armed forces."
10. "I'm feeling patriotic!" exclaimed Jesse. "Let's sing 'Yankee Doodle'!"

B., page 288
(Answers will vary. Students will satisfactorily complete this exercise if the dialogue is written in sentence form and has correct punctuation.)

CHAPTER 25: SPELLING

THE DICTIONARY
EXERCISE 1, page 290
1. se-ri-ous
2. armadillos
3. a measure of capacity for grain, fruits, and other things equal to eight quarts; to strike at and pick up with the beak; a stroke made with the beak
4. awoke or awaked
5. when it refers to the Roman god of love

EXERCISE 2, page 290
1. enrol
2. catalogue
3. hurray
4. whizz
5. judgement

SPELLING RULES
EXERCISE 3, page 291
1. shield
2. freight
3. pier
4. sleigh
5. yield
6. piece
7. review
8. weight
9. receive
10. friend

EXERCISE 4, page 292
1. exceeded
2. brief
3. their
4. leisurely
5. believed
6. either
7. Shielding
8. concede
9. friend
10. piece

PREFIXES AND SUFFIXES
EXERCISE 5, page 294
1. newness
2. really
3. unclear
4. overspend
5. finally
6. loudness
7. overripe
8. playfulness
9. friendliness
10. irregular
11. misspell
12. imperfect
13. heaviness
14. disable
15. informal
16. joyfully
17. steadily
18. incomplete
19. lastly
20. shyness

EXERCISE 6, page 294
1. noisily
2. believing
3. hopeful
4. strangest
5. grazing
6. pavement
7. politeness
8. wasteful
9. adorable
10. busily
11. amazing
12. hastily
13. measurement
14. courageous
15. driver
16. angrily
17. braver
18. littlest
19. changeable
20. careful

SUFFIXES
EXERCISE 7, page 295
1. dizziness
2. grinning
3. skidded
4. fresher
5. rustiest
6. keyed
7. multiplying
8. cheered
9. lazier
10. stayed

EXERCISE 8, page 296
1. rising
2. dripped
3. unusually
4. skidded
5. racing
6. cried
7. beginning
8. Worried
9. learned
10. paid

PLURALS OF NOUNS I
EXERCISE 9, page 297
1. dishes
2. pillows
3. reflexes
4. Pérezes
5. ranches
6. wishes
7. fields
8. monkeys
9. guesses
10. closets
11. benches
12. flashes
13. Martínezes
14. axes
15. dances
16. ideas
17. chimneys
18. harnesses
19. Joneses
20. dashes
21. candles
22. kisses
23. waltzes
24. rockets
25. stitches

EXERCISE 10, page 298
1. pen pals
2. libraries
3. handkerchiefs
4. mysteries
5. wives
6. coats-of-arms
7. victories
8. scarves or scarfs
9. staffs
10. subways
11. countries
12. Brodskys
13. journeys
14. melodies
15. goal posts
16. halves
17. boys
18. Sundays
19. galaxies
20. elves

PLURALS OF NOUNS II
EXERCISE 11, page 299
1. igloos
2. zeros or zeroes
3. sombreros
4. oxen
5. feet
6. deer
7. mottoes or mottos
8. trios
9. teeth
10. patios

EXERCISE 12, page 300
1. children
2. radios
3. pianos
4. cellos; banjos
5. piccolos
6. heroes
7. (correct)
8. echoes
9. holidays
10. sopranos

CHAPTER REVIEW
A., page 301
1. preceded
2. larger
3. height
4. easily
5. stitches
6. highways
7. amazing
8. children
9. sitting
10. leaves

B., page 301
1. mysterious; beautiful; reefs
2. lemons; potatoes
3. Providing; themselves
4. bodies
5. tiny; called
6. their; noticeable
7. octopuses or octopi
8. animals; inches
9. boneless; easily
10. enemies; hastily; proceed

C., page 302
(Answers will vary. Students' responses should show an understanding of spelling rules.)

ENGLISH WORKSHOP—FIRST COURSE

ANSWER KEY: Assessment Booklet

CHAPTER 10: THE SENTENCE

DIAGNOSTIC TEST, page 1

A.
1. *compl. s.*—My class, *compl. pred.*—visited an art museum last week, *simp. s.*—class, *v.*—visited
2. *compl. s.*—Michelangelo, *compl. pred.*—created beautiful works of art, *simp. s.*—Michelangelo, *v.*—created
3. *compl. s.*—He, *compl. pred.*—worked as a painter, sculptor, architect, and poet, *simp. s.*—He, *v.*—worked
4. *compl. s.*—This talented man, *compl. pred.*—painted the Sistine Chapel ceiling, *simp. s.*—man, *v.*—painted
5. *compl. s.*—Michelangelo's *Pietà*, *compl. pred.*—is a well-known and beautiful sculpture, *simp. s.*—*Pietà*, *v.*—is
6. *compl. s.*—My little brother and I, *compl. pred.*—rode a bus to the wildlife park, *simp. s.*—brother, I, *v.*—rode
7. *compl. s.*—My little brother, *compl. pred.*—was afraid of the crocodiles, *simp. s.*—brother, *v.*—was
8. *compl. s.*—Four crocodiles, *compl. pred.*—swam in a muddy pond, *simp. s.*—crocodiles, *v.*—swam
9. *compl. s.*—Crocodiles, *compl. pred.*—shed tears, *simp. s.*—Crocodiles, *v.*—shed
10. *compl. s.*—The tears, *compl. pred.*—wash away salt from their eyes, *simp. s.*—tears, *v.*—wash
11. *compl. s.*—That postcard and this poster, *compl. pred.*—show four sea lions, *simp. s.*—postcard, poster, *v.*—show
12. *compl. s.*—Some sea lions, *compl. pred.*—swim six thousand miles at a stretch, *simp. s.*—sea lions, *v.*—swim
13. *compl. s.*—Sea lions, *compl. pred.*—can be sunburned and seasick, *simp. s.*—sea lions, *v.*—can be
14. *compl. s.*—Male sea lions, *compl. pred.*—can go without food for three months, *simp. s.*—sea lions, *v.*—can go
15. *compl. s.*—The plump sea lions, *compl. pred.*—sat on rocks in front of the aquarium, *simp. s.*—sea lions, *v.*—sat

B.
16. dec., studied, visited
17. imp., listen, ask
18. exc., played, swam
19. dec., saw, photographed
20. inter., Can imagine, (can) appreciate

POSTTEST, page 2

A.
1. *compl. s.*—My class, *compl. pred.*—learned about the Ming dynasty of China, *simp. s.*—class, *v.*—learned
2. *compl. s.*—I, *compl. pred.*—always enjoy Mr. Zabel's history lectures, *simp. s.*—I, *v.*—enjoy
3. *compl. s.*—Thomas Edison, *compl. pred.*—invented the phonograph, the light bulb, and many other items, *simp. s.*—Thomas Edison, *v.*—invented
4. *compl. s.*—Abraham Lincoln, *compl. pred.*—became president in 1861, *simp. s.*—Abraham Lincoln, *v.*—became
5. *compl. s.*—Your body, *compl. pred.*—has 206 bones, *simp. s.*—body, *v.*—has
6. *compl. s.*—Some species of sharks, *compl. pred.*—grow new rows of teeth every week, *simp. s.*—species, *v.*—grow
7. *compl. s.*—About six hundred active volcanoes, *compl. pred.*—exist in the world, *simp. s.*—volcanoes, *v.*—exist
8. *compl. s.*—New Delhi and Calcutta, *compl. pred.*—are large cities in India, *simp. s.*—New Delhi, Calcutta, *v.*—are
9. *compl. s.*—The first Olympic games, *compl. pred.*—were in Greece, *simp. s.*—games, *v.*—were
10. *compl. s.*—The earth, *compl. pred.*—is 4.5 billion years old, *simp. s.*—earth, *v.*—is
11. *compl. s.*—A tsunami, *compl. pred.*—is a tidal wave, *simp. s.*—tsunami, *v.*—is
12. *compl. s.*—The legendary King Arthur, *compl. pred.*—pulled a sword from a stone, *simp. s.*—King Arthur, *v.*—pulled
13. *compl. s.*—My sister and I, *compl. pred.*—saw a dinosaur fossil at the museum, *simp. s.*—sister, I, *v.*—saw
14. *compl. s.*—Thomas Jefferson, *compl. pred.*—was the third president of the United States, *simp. s.*—Thomas Jefferson, *v.*—was
15. *compl. s.*—My family, *compl. pred.*—went on a whale watch last week, *simp. s.*—family, *v.*—went

B.
16. inter., Did have, (did) travel
17. imp., Read, decide
18. dec., lived, explored
19. exc., discovered, brought
20. dec., was captured, (was) placed

CHAPTER 11: PARTS OF SPEECH

DIAGNOSTIC TEST, page 3

A.
1. n.
2. pron. *or* adj.
3. adj.
4. adj.
5. n.
6. adj.
7. pron.
8. n.
9. pron.
10. adj.

B.
11. pron., Taschi
12. adj., Catskill Mountains
13. pron., Rip *or* adj., neighbors
14. adj., work
15. pron., Rip
16. adj., afternoon

37

17. pron., Strangers
18. adj., potion
19. adj., years
20. adj., man

POSTTEST, page 4
A.
1. adj.
2. pron. *or* adj.
3. n.
4. adj.
5. adj.
6. pron.
7. n.
8. adj.
9. pron.
10. n.

B.
11. adj., instruments
12. pron., sister *or* adj., band
13. adj., drums
14. pron., steel drums
15. adj., term
16. adj., islands
17. adj., barrels
18. pron., Musicians *or* adj., creativity
19. adj., instrument
20. adj., beans

CHAPTER 12: PARTS OF SPEECH

DIAGNOSTIC TEST, page 5
A.
1. v., linking
2. intj.
3. v., linking
4. v., action
5. prep.
6. intj.
7. v., action
8. conj.
9. prep.
10. conj.
11. v., helping
12. conj.
13. prep.
14. conj.
15. v., helping

B.
ADVERB	WORD MODIFIED
16. uniquely	talented
17. often	made
18. slowly	dried
19. carefully	studied
20. very	ancient

POSTTEST, page 6
A.
1. conj.
2. v., linking
3. intj.
4. v., action
5. intj.
6. v., linking
7. prep.
8. v., action
9. conj.
10. prep.
11. v., helping
12. prep.
13. prep.
14. conj.
15. v., helping

B.
ADVERB	WORD MODIFIED
16. regularly	Do feel
17. often	wondered
18. more easily	easily study
19. quietly	sat
20. very	different

CHAPTER 13: COMPLEMENTS

DIAGNOSTIC TEST, page 7
A.
1. p.n.
2. d.o.
3. p.n.
4. p.a.
5. i.o.
6. p.a.
7. p.n.
8. d.o.
9. d.o.
10. p.n.

B.
11. i.o., me; d.o., map
12. p.n., region
13. p.a., cold
14. d.o., challenges
15. i.o., me; d.o., chapter
16. d.o., clothing, tents
17. d.o., homes
18. p.n., igloos
19. d.o., heat; p.a., warm
20. p.a., different

POSTTEST, page 8
A.
1. d.o.
2. p.a.
3. i.o.
4. p.n.
5. d.o.
6. p.a.
7. i.o.
8. d.o.
9. p.a.
10. p.n.

B.
11. p.a., small, overcrowded
12. d.o., school
13. i.o., them; d.o., money
14. d.o., school
15. d.o., them
16. p.a., certain
17. d.o., school year
18. d.o., opportunity
19. d.o., schools; i.o., teachers; d.o., money
20. p.n., state

CHAPTER 14: THE PHRASE

DIAGNOSTIC TEST, page 9
A.
1. adj., of your brain, size
2. adv., to your bones, are joined
3. adj., of your body, organ
4. adv., during the year 1835, was born
5. adj., of a volcano, model
6. adj., about pride, speeches
7. adv., with their hind feet, taste
8. adv., into the sun, would fit
9. adv., For the school's chorus concert, will make
10. adj., of the past, computers

B.
11. part. phr., Researching artists
12. v. phr., was born
13. inf. phr., to paint
14. v. phr., had attended
15. inf. phr., to experiment with different themes and colors

16. part. phr., interested in circus themes
17. part. phr., Using bits of paper, metal, and other materials
18. inf. phr., to create stage sets for Sergei Diaghilev's ballet company
19. part. phr., Admired by many other artists
20. v. phr., has been called

POSTTEST, page 10
A.
1. adj., of many countries, flags
2. adv., about sculpture, is learning
3. adv., in oranges, is found
4. adv., from Russia, purchased
5. adv., In 1931, became
6. adv., in Mexico City, was born
7. adv., around the indoor track, jogged
8. adj., of nature, photographs
9. adj., near the boat, shark
10. adj., about Frankenstein's monster, novel

B.
11. inf. phr., to get equal rights
12. inf. phr., to be passed
13. v. phr., had resulted
14. part. phr., Angered by the prejudices
15. inf. phr., to attend school together
16. v. phr., were treated
17. v. phr., had begun
18. part. phr., Riding the bus one day
19. inf. phr., to give up her seat to a white man
20. v. phr., was arrested

CHAPTER 15:
THE CLAUSE

DIAGNOSTIC TEST, page 11
A.
1. indep.
2. sub.
3. indep.
4. indep.
5. sub.
6. indep.
7. indep.
8. sub.
9. indep.
10. sub.
11. indep.
12. sub.
13. indep.
14. sub.
15. sub.

B.
16. adv., Before I left the library
17. adj., who cares about the rights of children
18. adj., that works to protect all children
19. adv., After she graduated from law school
20. adv., Because she is such an energetic children's rights worker

POSTTEST, page 12
A.
1. indep.
2. sub.
3. sub.
4. indep.
5. indep.
6. sub.
7. indep.
8. sub.
9. sub.
10. indep.
11. sub.
12. indep.
13. sub.
14. sub.
15. indep.

B.
16. adv., When early astronomers explained the solar system
17. adv., If you read books on this subject
18. adj., who was a famous astronomer
19. adj., that Tycho Brahe proposed
20. adj., whose ideas were correct

CHAPTER 16:
SENTENCE STRUCTURE

DIAGNOSTIC TEST, page 13
A.

INDEP. CL.	SUB. CL.
1. The trees did not bear fruit	that were planted last year
2. An earthquake shook the town several buildings were destroyed	
3. Roland could see the distant mountains	If he looked through the window of his bedroom
4. I felt terrific today	because I had a good night's sleep
5. the football game will be postponed until tomorrow	If it rains
6. My grandfather made most of our furniture	who is a carpenter
7. This summer, Latoya and her sister are taking a course at the Woods Hole Oceanographic Institution	
8. The dishes must be packed carefully they might break	
9. We brought our ice skates the lake was not frozen	
10. Please turn off the lights in the living room	before you leave

B.
11. simp.
12. cx.
13. comp.
14. cx.
15. simp.
16. comp.
17. cx.
18. cx.
19. simp.
20. comp.

POSTTEST, page 14
A.

INDEP. CL.	SUB. CL.
1. John Bartlett published the first edition of *Familiar Quotations* in 1855	who was born in Plymouth, Massachusetts
2. For thousands of years, all books were copied by hand	
3. Matsu went to bed early she was very tired	
4. Is there enough gasoline in the tank should we refuel at the next gas station	

39

5. he also wrote many sonnets — Although Shakespeare is most famous for his plays

6. At the party, Una wore the dress — that her grandmother had made

7. Rudy washed the car — Phoebe polished it

8. the president sat down — After she introduced the speaker

9. I could not finish the job — Because I did not have the materials

10. Any student will receive a scholarship — who scores high on the test

11. Jerome brought the books — that you ordered

12. She did not seek the position — she accepted it willingly

13. No one knew the answer to the last question

14. The officer blew his whistle — the cars stopped

15. we canceled our trip — After we received the telegram

B.
16. simp.
17. cx.
18. cx.
19. simp.
20. comp.

CHAPTER 17: AGREEMENT

DIAGNOSTIC TEST, page 15

A.
1. were
2. Doesn't
3. are
4. play
5. (correct)
6. seems
7. study
8. is
9. (correct)
10. meets
11. are
12. grazes
13. knows
14. Do
15. (correct)

B.
16. their
17. their
18. his or her
19. her
20. (correct)

POSTTEST, page 16

A.
1. belongs
2. are
3. was
4. her
5. their
6. was
7. Do
8. attends
9. hangs
10. is
11. his
12. grows
13. its
14. Are
15. checks

B.

WORDS UNDERLINED	CORRECT FORMS
16. was	were
17. (correct)	
18. their	his or her

19. is — are
20. has — have

CHAPTER 18: USING VERBS CORRECTLY

DIAGNOSTIC TEST, page 17

A.
1. sitting
2. raised
3. laying
4. rise
5. lay
6. set
7. rise
8. sitting
9. laid
10. raise

B.

VERBS UNDERLINED	CORRECT FORMS
11. gone	went
12. costed	cost
13. (correct)	
14. brung	brought
15. sit	sat
16. seen	saw
17. done	did
18. come	came
19. sung	sang
20. stoled	stole

POSTTEST, page 18

A.
1. sitting
2. rose
3. lying
4. lay
5. set
6. rise
7. laid
8. set
9. risen
10. laid

B.

VERBS UNDERLINED	CORRECT FORMS
11. goed	went
12. begun	began
13. (correct)	
14. rode	ridden
15. seen	saw
16. leads	led
17. done	did
18. winned	won
19. stands	stood
20. bust	burst

CHAPTER 19: USING PRONOUNS CORRECTLY

DIAGNOSTIC TEST, page 19

A.
1. me
2. he
3. her
4. he
5. him and her
6. me
7. them
8. Who
9. us
10. Who
11. whom
12. themselves
13. we
14. himself
15. We

B.

	PRONOUNS UNDERLINED	CORRECT FORMS
16.	theirselves	themselves
17.	they	them
18.	I	me
19.	her	she
20.	(correct)	

POSTTEST, page 20
A.

1. she
2. me
3. he
4. me
5. whom
6. them
7. himself
8. Whom
9. us
10. Who
11. us
12. themselves
13. we
14. We
15. Whom

B.

	PRONOUNS UNDERLINED	CORRECT FORMS
16.	we	us
17.	I	me
18.	(correct)	
19.	hisself	himself
20.	him	he

CHAPTER 20:
USING MODIFIERS CORRECTLY

DIAGNOSTIC TEST, page 21
A.

(Answers will vary. Possible responses are given.)
1. Driving his truck across the desert, he spotted a bald eagle.
2. Riding down the hill, I got dust in my eyes.
3. Chang couldn't remember the dog's name.
4. C
5. That was the worst storm that ever hit the island of Guam.
6. Yesterday I was sick, but today I feel better.
7. When the gate opens, move quickly.
8. He gave the food in the saucer to the cat.
9. For people living in the city, noise is often a problem.
10. He saw a huge black crow nesting at the top of the spruce tree.

B.

11. more
12. hottest
13. didn't mind
14. least
15. quickly
16. bad
17. worse
18. gently
19. better
20. fresh

POSTTEST, page 22
A.

(Answers will vary. Possible responses are given.)
1. Trying on my new shoes, I noticed that they pinched.
2. My uncle gave tropical fish with long, feathery fins to my cousins.
3. I think this was the coldest day we've had all winter.
4. Holding her camera very still, Betty took pictures of a rhinoceros.
5. Please sit quietly during the speech.
6. If you leave the rolls in the oven a few more minutes, they will be warmer.
7. Henri paints well, and Simone takes good photographs.
8. Denise couldn't find the new Billy Joel album anywhere.
9. This is the highest mountain I have ever climbed.
10. C

B.

11. best
12. made
13. more
14. most popular
15. lighter
16. most outstanding
17. most
18. frequently
19. more
20. closely

CHAPTER 21:
A GLOSSARY OF USAGE

DIAGNOSTIC TEST, page 23
A.

1. already
2. ought
3. well
4. its
5. as
6. Try to
7. who
8. Who's
9. You're
10. a word that

B.

	ERROR	CORRECTION
11.	excepted	accepted
12.	alot	a lot
13.	learned	taught
14.	taken	brought
15.	between	among
16.	less	fewer
17.	real	rather
18.	where	that
19.	good	well
20.	would of	would have

POSTTEST, page 24
A.

1. well
2. Whose
3. who
4. except
5. take
6. must have
7. It's
8. as
9. all right
10. taught

B.

	ERROR	CORRECTION
11.	good	well
12.	alot	a lot
13.	theirselves	themselves
14.	real	rather
15.	Its	It's
16.	Try and	Try to
17.	Your	You're
18.	Between	Among
19.	excepted	accepted
20.	Those	This *or* That

41

CHAPTER 22: CAPITAL LETTERS

DIAGNOSTIC TEST, page 25

A.
1. a.
2. b.
3. a.
4. a.
5. b.
6. b.
7. b.
8. b.
9. b.
10. a.
11. b.
12. a.
13. b.
14. b.

B.
15. American
16. Native American, New York
17. art school
18. earth
19. Smithsonian Institution, D. C.
20. French, Paul Cézanne, Henri Matisse

POSTTEST, page 26

A.
1. a.
2. b.
3. a.
4. b.
5. b.
6. b.
7. a.
8. b.
9. a.
10. b.
11. a.
12. a.
13. b.
14. a.

B.
15. Cuban American
16. career, band, Miami Sound Machine
17. leader, Emilio Estefan
18. songs, Spanish, English
19. star
20. London Symphony Orchestra

CHAPTER 23: PUNCTUATION

DIAGNOSTIC TEST, page 27

A.
1. boot, Harriet!
2. James, tonight?
3. B.C.?
4. 5:32 P.M.
5. bird, jay,
6. Al, heard, IRS.
7. puddles;
8. follows: Weston,
9. 7:40 A.M. 1993, Waco,
10. Ohio; Dallas, Texas;
11. you, Dr. Goldblum,
12. follows: St., Houston,

B.
[13] Many people in our neighborhood joined together to form a club, the 12th Avenue Players. [14] It all started on June 1, 1991, when a nearby neighborhood group, the East End Jazz Band, had a festival. [15] Several people from my neighborhood went; all of them came back really excited. [16] Eager to try our luck at forming our own neighborhood group, we called a meeting the following day. [17] We discussed our ideas, we decided to create a club, and we nominated officers. [18] The rest, as you know, is history; the 12th Avenue Players are known all over the city now. [19] Our current officers are as follows: Otis Taylor, president; Marya Wood, treasurer; and Drew Roberts, talent coordinator. [20] Our next play, Thornton Wilder's *Our Town*, will open on October 3.

POSTTEST, page 28

A.
1. follows: Bellevue, VT 18902.
2. airport, 6:41 P.M.
3. Oh, no! field, Jim! (*or* .)
4. Dr. García, know, Mt., Hospital.
5. F., Ave.?
6. in, Mrs. Robbe, guest, Mr., C. Gilson.
7. B.C.?
8. items: bread, milk, lettuce.
9. important; faith, it.
10. 4:49 morning, Boise, Idaho.
11. Canton, Ohio; Booth, Iowa; Spring, Texas.
12. 2, 1993?

B.
[13] Are you ready to hear the exciting news that my sister Rosa and I heard on July 5, 1993? [14] We received a letter from Ms. Vanessa Goldblatt, an official with a student-exchange program. [15] We ripped open the letter as soon as it arrived, for we had been waiting for it since May 1993. [16] As my sister read it, I tried to peek over her shoulder; the suspense was killing me! [17] Well, the news was fantastic. [18] In three weeks, Rosa and I will fly to Lima, Peru, to begin our year as foreign students in South America! [19] From Lima we will travel to the following cities: Buenos Aires, Argentina; Santiago, Chile; and Bogotá, Colombia.
[20] As soon as I get to Lima, I'll send you my address there; please write to me!

CHAPTER 24: PUNCTUATION

DIAGNOSTIC TEST, page 29

A.
1. b.
2. b.
3. a.
4. b.
5. a.
6. a.
7. b.
8. b.
9. a.
10. b.
11. a.
12. b.
13. b.
14. b.

B.
[15] Tim called Kate. "Will you help me make posters for the election?" he asked.
[16] "Sure," Kate answered. "Just let me finish this book."
[17] "Aren't you reading Michael Crichton's dinosaur book, <u>Jurassic Park</u>?" he asked.
[18] "No," she said. "I've finished that. Now I'm reading another book by Michael Crichton. It's called <u>The Great Train Robbery.</u> But I'll stop now and come over to help you."
[19] Together they made posters. "Are you sure there's an <u>a</u> in the word <u>treasurer</u>?" Tim asked. "You can't hear any <u>a</u> in there."
[20] "Yes," said Kate. "Its first four letters are <u>t, r, e, a.</u>"

POSTTEST, page 30

A.
1. b.
2. b.
3. a.
4. b.
5. a.
6. b.
7. a.
8. a.
9. b.
10. b.
11. b.
12. b.
13. a.
14. a.

B.
[15] Rosalia, Toni, and Pat were studying for a geography test. "Let's review the major river ports in the United States," Pat suggested.
[16] "I've got our book, <u>Lands and Peoples,</u> right here if we need it," said Toni.
[17] "Great," said Rosalia. "First, there's New Orleans."
[18] "Yes," said Pat, "it's where the Mississippi River empties into the Gulf of Mexico."

[19] "I'll make a chart," Rosalia said. "How do you spell the word <u>Mississippi</u>?"

[20] "There are four <u>s</u>'s, four <u>i</u>'s, and two <u>p</u>'s," Pat answered.

CHAPTER 25: SPELLING

DIAGNOSTIC TEST, page 31

A.
1. friends
2. happiness
3. Courageous
4. grinning
5. factories
6. lilies
7. studios
8. geese
9. height
10. peaches
11. useless
12. hoped
13. (correct)
14. (correct)
15. truly

B.
16. thief
17. street
18. unbelievable
19. proceeding
20. leaves

POSTTEST, page 32

A.
1. sitting
2. holidays
3. amazing
4. mischief
5. measurements
6. skidded
7. hastily
8. ranches
9. waltzes
10. foreign
11. mysteries
12. echoes
13. teeth
14. hoping
15. (correct)

B.
16. plentiful
17. exceeded
18. watches
19. truly
20. stitches